AMERICAN HISTORY THROUGH MAPS

meat

D1216011

THIS BOOK IS THE PROPERTY OF:

STATE_____
PROVINCE_____
COUNTY_____
PARISH_____
SCHOOL DISTRICT_____
OTHER_____

Book No. _____
Enter information in
one of the spaces
to the left as
instructed

ISSUED TO	Year Used	CONDITION	
		ISSUED	RETURNED
....	....		
....	....		
....	....		
....	....		

PUPILS to whom this textbook is issued must not write on any page or mark any part of it in any way, consumable textbooks excepted.

1. Teachers should see that the pupil's name is clearly written in ink in the spaces above in every book issued.
2. The following terms should be used in recording the condition of the book: New; Good; Fair; Poor; Bad.

HAMMOND®
INCORPORATED
MAPLEWOOD, NEW JERSEY   07040-1396

L.C. 84-81348   ISBN 0-8437-7435-5   PRINTED IN THE UNITED STATES OF AMERICA

CONTENTS

PATTERNS AND EVENTS

MAPS OF AMERICAN HISTORY

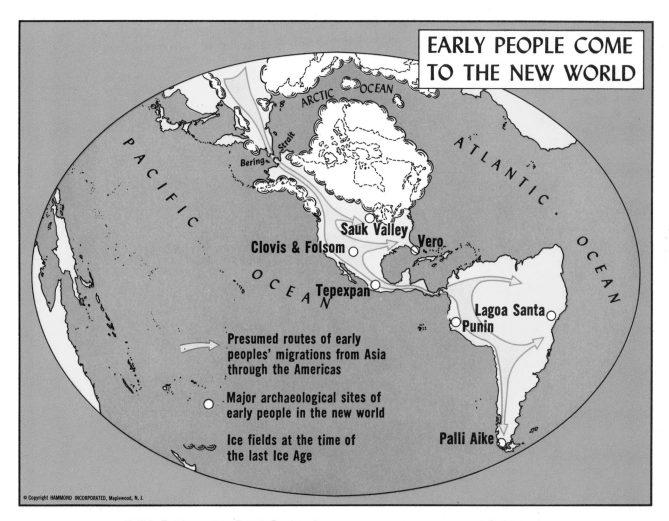

EARLY PEOPLE COME TO THE NEW WORLD

MIGRATIONS TO THE NEW WORLD

Unfortunately, the first people to come to the New World did not leave us any written records. They left no books telling where they came from and where they went after they got here. Fortunately, they did leave another kind of record. At the places where they settled, they left remains of their lives — bones, tools, pottery, weapons.

Scientists called archaeologists use these remains as evidence. From this evidence they gather clues about who these early people were, where they traveled, and how they lived.

Archaeologists have determined that these people came from Asia at least 12,000 years ago. They were groups of hunters who came from Siberia to Alaska in search of game. Over the years, they traveled deeper and deeper into the American continents.

From the evidence these people left, we know that some of them gave up hunting and started to gather berries and nuts. Others fished for their food. Some discovered how to grow crops. Many settled in villages. They spoke many different languages.

1. Consult an encyclopedia. In two paragraphs, describe the Ice Age and its effects on the topography of North America.
2. Find a modern map of North and South America in your classroom atlas or in an atlas from your school library. Then from that source, determine in what modern-day state or country you would find the following places shown on the map above: Vero, Tepexpan, and Palli Aike.

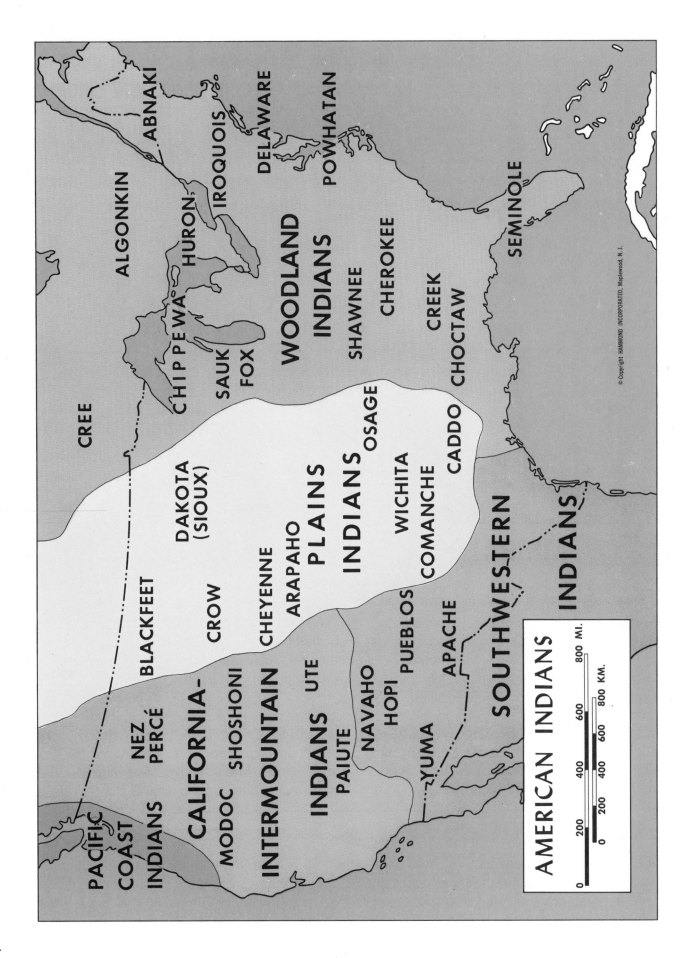

PACIFIC COAST INDIANS

CREE

ALGONKIN

ABNAKI

CHIPPEWA

HURON

IROQUOIS

DELAWARE

POWHATAN

WOODLAND INDIANS

SEMINOLE

SAUK

FOX

SHAWNEE

CHEROKEE

CREEK

CHOCTAW

NEZ PERCÉ

BLACKFEET

CROW

DAKOTA (SIOUX)

CHEYENNE

ARAPAHO

PLAINS INDIANS

OSAGE

WICHITA

COMANCHE

CADDO

CALIFORNIA-

MODOC

SHOSHONI

INTERMOUNTAIN INDIANS

UTE

PAIUTE

NAVAHO

HOPI

PUEBLOS

APACHE

YUMA

SOUTHWESTERN INDIANS

© Copyright HAMMOND INCORPORATED, Maplewood, N. J.

AMERICAN INDIANS

0   200   400   600   800 MI.

0   200   400   600   800 KM.

4

THE FIRST AMERICANS

When Christopher Columbus landed in the Bahamas in 1492, he thought he was in the Indies — islands off the southeastern coast of Asia. Therefore, he called the people there *Indians*. This mistake was soon discovered, but Europeans continued to use the name *Indian*.

There were about 300 different tribes in North America at the time of Columbus. Each tribe had a different name and different customs. (A tribe is a group of families that speaks the same language, shares the same lands, and has similar ways of life.)

The North American tribes are often divided into the five major groups shown in the map on page 4. The geography of the region in which each group lived was important in determining how they lived.

In the east were the Woodland Indians. These were the Indians the early American colonists met first. They were both farmers and hunters. Most Woodland Indians lived in small villages. They raised maize, squash, and beans. In the forests, they hunted deer and other game with bows and arrows. They picked wild berries and gathered nuts. Birchbark canoes enabled them to travel swiftly over lakes and streams on fishing, trading, and warring missions. The most advanced of the Woodland Indians were the Iroquois of the northeast. Their democratic form of government greatly impressed the colonists.

The Plains Indians were wandering hunters who traveled over the open grasslands in search of the buffalo. These tribes did not have permanent homes. Their temporary dwelling was the tepee — a tent of wooden poles and animal skins that could be put up easily and quickly. The Plains Indians hunted on foot until the Spaniards brought the horse to the Americas. After that, the horse became their most important possession.

The Indians of the southwest were farmers and city builders. The land of this area is dry, but people were able to grow abundant crops of maize and squash. They trapped water from flooding rivers and used it to irrigate their crops. Most Southwestern Indians lived in villages, or pueblos. Such groups as the Hopi built mudbrick houses several stories high in cliff walls or on flat rocky areas. They made beautiful pottery and jewelry.

The California-Intermountain Indians lived a simple yet difficult life. Most of this area is barren, and tribes lived by gathering seeds and nuts. They spent most of their time looking for food, and had little time for developing many crafts. But they were expert basketmakers.

In the northwest, the Pacific Coast Indians lived in an area that had a mild climate and was rich in natural resources. The sea swarmed with cod, halibut, and sea otter. In the spring, rivers were filled with salmon. Thick forests provided timber for great houses, seagoing canoes, and totem poles. Most of the tribes of this region were wealthy. They made things of great beauty and developed complex ways of life. Many celebrations were held to show others their great wealth. Sometimes the hosts gave much of this wealth to their guests.

1. On a sheet of tracing paper, trace the map on page 4 and show the boundaries of the five colored divisions of Indian tribes. Then, using pictures or symbols, indicate the chief occupations of each tribe.

2. On a sheet of paper, answer the following: In what direction did the Seminoles live from the Utes? The Modocs from the Apaches? The Dakotas from the Comanches? Be as precise as possible in designating all directions.

3. Are there any things in your life that reflect the Indians' culture? Explain in a paragraph.

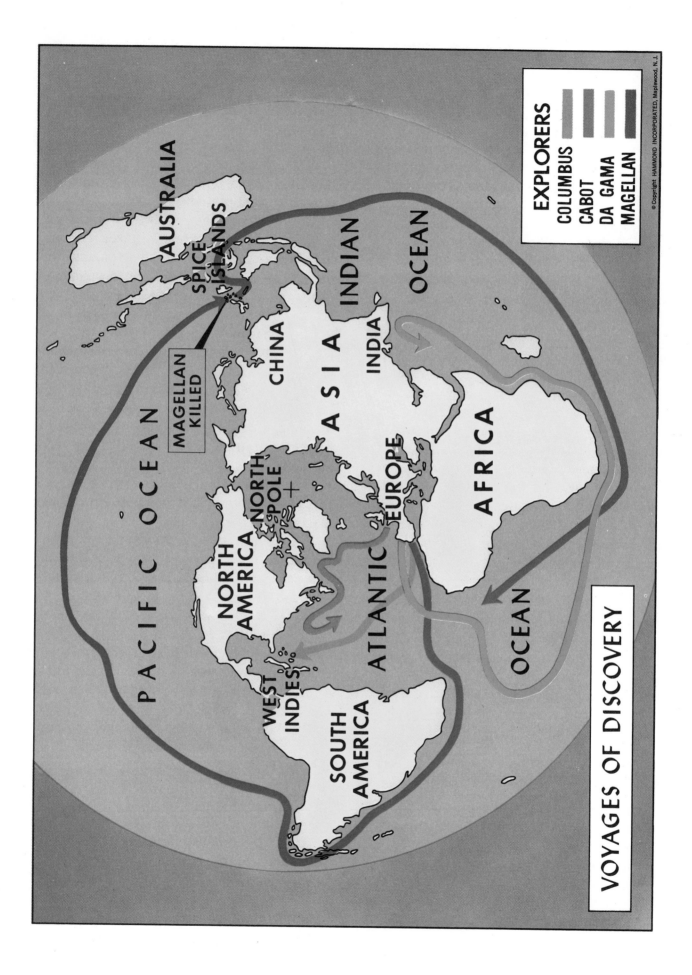

VOYAGES OF DISCOVERY

VOYAGES OF DISCOVERY

Europe of the 1400s was hungry for the goods of Asia. Europeans wanted pepper from India, spices from the East Indies, and silk from China. For centuries, caravans had brought these goods overland from Asia. But the trip was costly and difficult.

Many Europeans began to think that a water route would be cheaper and easier. Soon three nations — Spain, England, and Portugal — started the quest for a new "all-water" route to the Far East.

The rulers of Spain hired Christopher Columbus, an Italian navigator, to sail under their flag. He had convinced them that he could reach Asia by traveling west. In the summer of 1492, he set sail. On October 12, he thought he had reached his goal. But he had not landed in Asia. He had landed on one of the islands that are now called the Bahamas. Even though Columbus made three more voyages west, he never realized he had found a New World — and not Asia.

England also tried a western route to Asia. The English sent John Cabot, another Italian navigator, and his son Sebastian to search for it. These explorers knew about Columbus's voyages, and they decided to take a more northern route. In 1497, they landed on the eastern coast of either Newfoundland or Nova Scotia. The Cabots realized that they had not reached Asia. They had landed on an unknown continent, and they claimed it for England.

Portugal had been trying to find a water route to Asia by sailing around Africa. After several attempts had failed, Vasco da Gama succeeded. He sailed south, went around Africa's Cape of Good Hope, and reached India in 1498. Portugal had found an all-water route to the riches of the Far East. As a result, the Portuguese gained a control over the spice trade that lasted 100 years.

In order to break Portugal's control, Spain again sent out a westward expedition. By this time, the Spaniards knew that Columbus had not reached Asia. They knew that ships would have to bypass the continents of the New World and sail farther on.

In 1519, Ferdinand Magellan began this voyage for Spain. With five ships, he headed west. Then he turned and sailed down along the eastern coast of South America and around its southern tip. Next, he sailed across the Pacific Ocean until he reached the Philippine Islands. It was here in 1521 that Magellan was killed. But his ships went on, continuing westward through the Indian Ocean and around the southern tip of Africa. From there they sailed up the coast of Africa and home to Spain. Only one ship with a cargo full of spices and a crew of 18 made it back in 1522.

In all, the voyage had taken three years. It revealed for the first time the extent of the world and the position of its continents and oceans.

1. What countries sent explorers to find a water route to Asia? Name the explorer(s) who were sent by each of these countries. List your answers on a sheet of paper.
2. On a sheet of paper, discuss in two or more paragraphs what prompted European nations to find a water route to Asia. Include the advantages of this type of route as well as the disadvantages.
3. On a sheet of paper, answer the following questions: Which country was the first to send a successful expedition to the Far East? How did this country benefit from the voyage?
4. After tracing Magellan's route on page 6, write one or two well-constructed paragraphs which discuss why he followed this route, the bodies of water he traveled, the continents he neared, and the importance of his discovery.

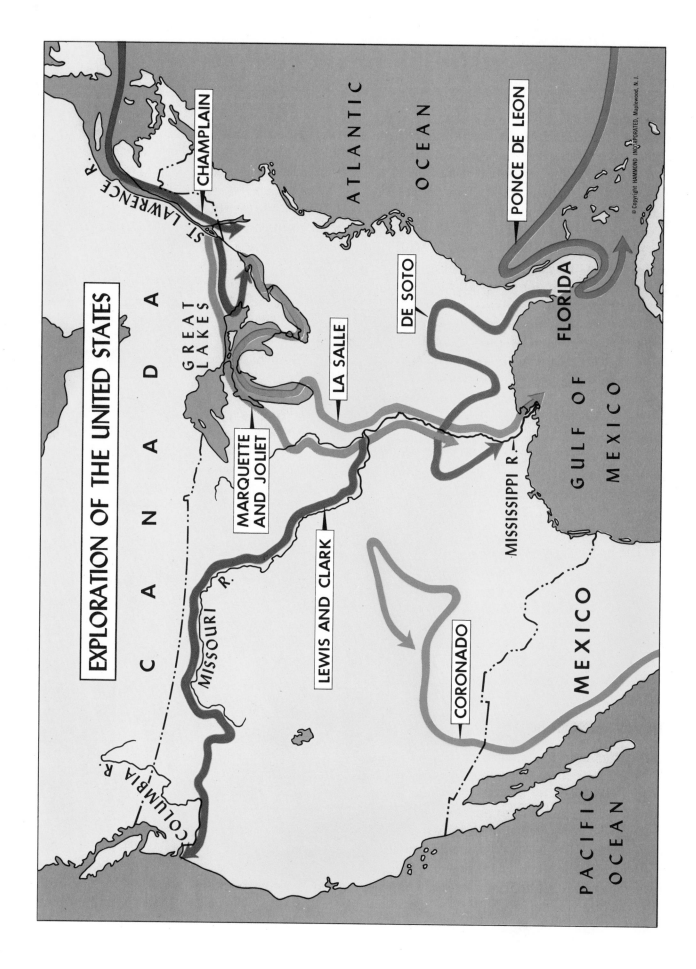

EXPLORATION OF THE UNITED STATES

CANADA

GREAT LAKES

ST. LAWRENCE R.

CHAMPLAIN

ATLANTIC OCEAN

PONCE DE LEON

FLORIDA

DE SOTO

LA SALLE

MARQUETTE AND JOLIET

MISSOURI R.

LEWIS AND CLARK

CORONADO

MISSISSIPPI R.

GULF OF MEXICO

MEXICO

COLUMBIA R.

PACIFIC OCEAN

© Copyright HAMMOND INCORPORATED, Maplewood, N. J.

EXPLORATION OF THE UNITED STATES

People from several nations explored North America, and they did so for many different reasons.

Spain was the first nation to send explorers inland into what is now the United States. Among the first Spaniards to come was Ponce de Leon in 1513. He had heard that there was a "Fountain of Youth" in a place called "Bimini," and he wanted to find it. His search took him to what he called "Florida." Ponce de Leon explored much of the coast, but he never found the fountain. Instead, when he returned eight years later to set up a colony, an Indian arrow wounded him. He died soon afterwards.

About 25 years later, two more Spaniards — Hernando de Soto and Francisco Coronado — led explorations into the continent. They too were searching for something they had heard stories about. De Soto was trying to find the gold of Florida. Coronado was seeking the "Seven Cities of Cibola," which legend said were paved with gold and decorated with precious gems. Neither man ever found what he was searching for, but De Soto discovered the Mississippi River. Coronado's expedition found the Grand Canyon.

France also wanted to learn more about North America. The French were interested in establishing settlements in the New World and in sharing in its wealth of furs and fish. The French king sent Samuel de Champlain to explore the new land and find good places to establish settlements. In 1608, he founded the city of Quebec. Later he built a trading post in what is now Montreal.

Seventy years later, two Frenchmen explored deep inland. Father Jacques Marquette and Louis Joliet traveled westward through the Great Lakes and paddled down the Mississippi. They hoped that the river would turn westward and flow into the Pacific Ocean. When they were sure it would not, they turned back. A few years later, their countryman Robert de La Salle completed the trip down the Mississippi. He claimed the whole valley surrounding it for France.

More than a century later, still another nation sent explorers deep into North America. The newly formed United States government wanted to find out about the unknown lands that lay to the west. President Thomas Jefferson chose his secretary, Meriwether Lewis, and a former army officer, William Clark, to head the expedition. There were several reasons for the trip. The explorers were to record scientific information about the western lands. They were also to find a route to the Pacific. Finally, they were to pave the way for settlers to follow.

With a young Indian woman, Sacajawea, as their guide, Lewis and Clark traveled across more than half the continent. By the time they returned, they had accomplished most of what they had set out to do. They had made friends with some of the Indians of the area. They had paved the way for fur traders and other explorers. American settlers soon began to stream into the Missouri and Columbia valleys.

1. Study the seven routes found on page 8. On a separate sheet of paper, describe the directions each exploration took from start to finish. Be as specific as possible in your description.
2. Compare the maps on pages 4 and 8. On a separate sheet of paper, indicate which explorer(s) might have encountered any of the following tribes on their journeys: Nez Percé, Seminoles, Pueblos, or the Iroquois.
3. In two or three paragraphs, describe the Lewis and Clark expedition. Be sure to include the purposes of their journey, the land and water routes they followed, and the results of their exploration. If you wish, consult an encyclopedia.

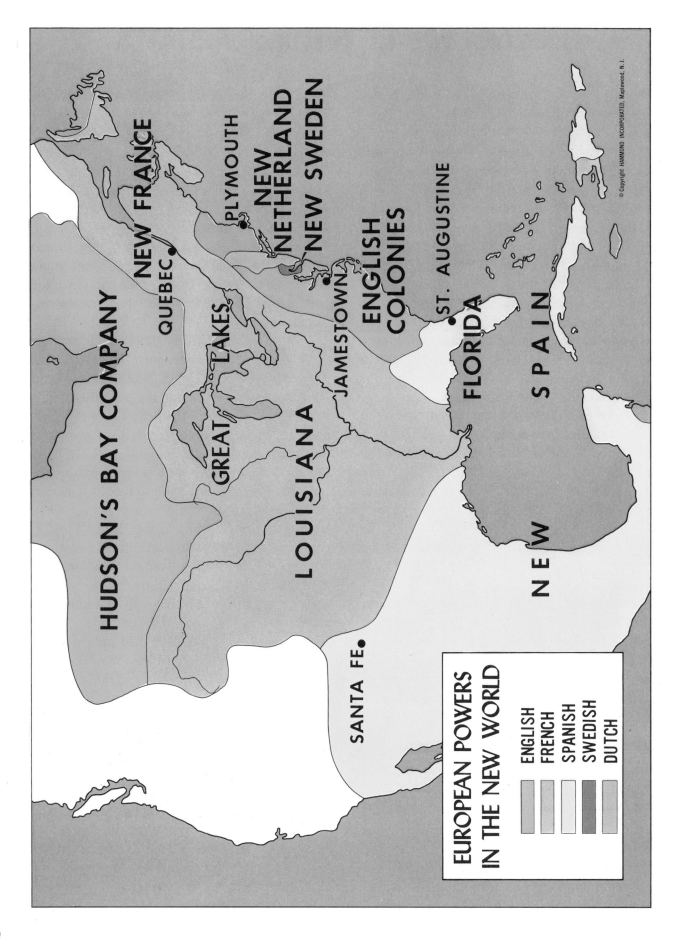

EUROPEAN POWERS
IN THE NEW WORLD

HUDSON'S BAY COMPANY

NEW FRANCE
QUEBEC

GREAT LAKES

PLYMOUTH

NEW NETHERLAND
NEW SWEDEN

JAMESTOWN

ENGLISH COLONIES

LOUISIANA

FLORIDA
ST. AUGUSTINE

SANTA FE

NEW SPAIN

ENGLISH
FRENCH
SPANISH
SWEDISH
DUTCH

EUROPEAN POWERS IN THE NEW WORLD

European powers claimed vast land areas in the New World as their own. They based their claims on the explorations they had backed. For example, you have already seen that France claimed all of the Mississippi River Valley because their explorer La Salle had traveled through it. Spain claimed Florida and the Southwest on the basis of De Leon's and Coronado's explorations.

The map on page 10 shows the areas European nations claimed in the 1660s. But these nations were not content to stay within their own territories. They wanted to gain control over lands claimed by other nations. The first nations to lose their lands were the Netherlands and Sweden. England wanted their colonies and was strong enough to take them away without firing a shot. New Netherland and New Sweden soon became part of England's territories.

1. After looking at the map on page 10, answer the following questions on a sheet of paper: Whose claims were farthest north, south, east, and west?
2. Compare the map on page 10 and the map of the United States on the inside front cover and decide which nation you feel had claim to the territory with the most beneficial physical features. Then in a paragraph or two, explain how you arrived at your decision.

FRENCH AND INDIAN WAR
MAP—PAGE 12

The English colonists yearned to move farther west to the Ohio Valley. The land there teemed with valuable fur-bearing animals, and the many rivers and lakes made transportation by water possible for long distances. But France claimed this land.

In 1754, tension between the two nations sparked the French and Indian War. This war was so named because the English fought against both the French and their allies, the Indians.

The war began badly for the English. General Edward Braddock and his army attacked the French at Fort Duquesne. Braddock's redcoated soldiers were easy targets for the French and Indians hidden behind trees and rocks. Half of the general's troops were killed, wounded, or captured, and Braddock himself was killed.

But in the next few years, the tide of battle turned for the English. In 1758, General John Amherst and his troops captured Louisbourg, an important French port. Louisbourg gave the English a base from which they could send their navy to cut off French supply ships. In 1759, General James Wolfe and his army captured France's most important settlement, Quebec, in a spectacular surprise attack. They had climbed 300 feet up a steep cliff at night and had marched silently to the battlefield to wait for the French.

By 1763, the war was over. England had won land east of the Mississippi River from the French.

1. Look at the map on page 12 and note where Quebec and Louisbourg are located. Explain how capturing these two places helped to secure an English victory.
2. Consult an encyclopedia to discover how French territory was distributed after the war. Then draw a map showing what nation gained what area as a result.

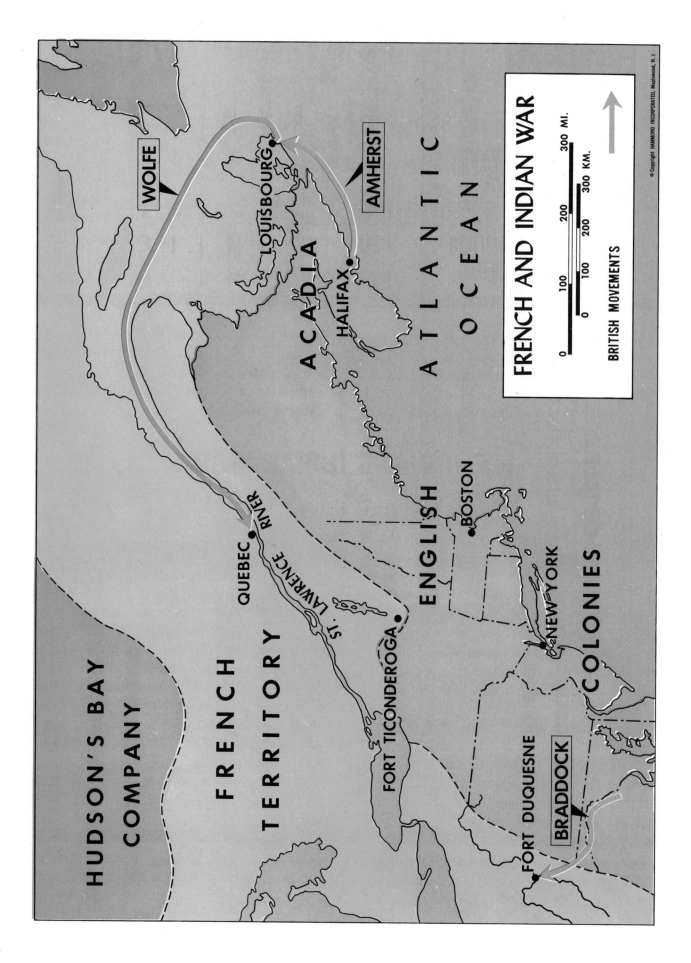

FRENCH AND INDIAN WAR

WOLFE

AMHERST

LOUISBOURG

ACADIA

HALIFAX

ATLANTIC OCEAN

BOSTON

ENGLISH

NEW YORK

COLONIES

QUEBEC

ST. LAWRENCE RIVER

FORT TICONDEROGA

FRENCH

TERRITORY

HUDSON'S BAY COMPANY

FORT DUQUESNE

BRADDOCK

BRITISH MOVEMENTS

300 MI.

300 KM.

© Copyright HAMMOND INCORPORATED, Maplewood, N.J.

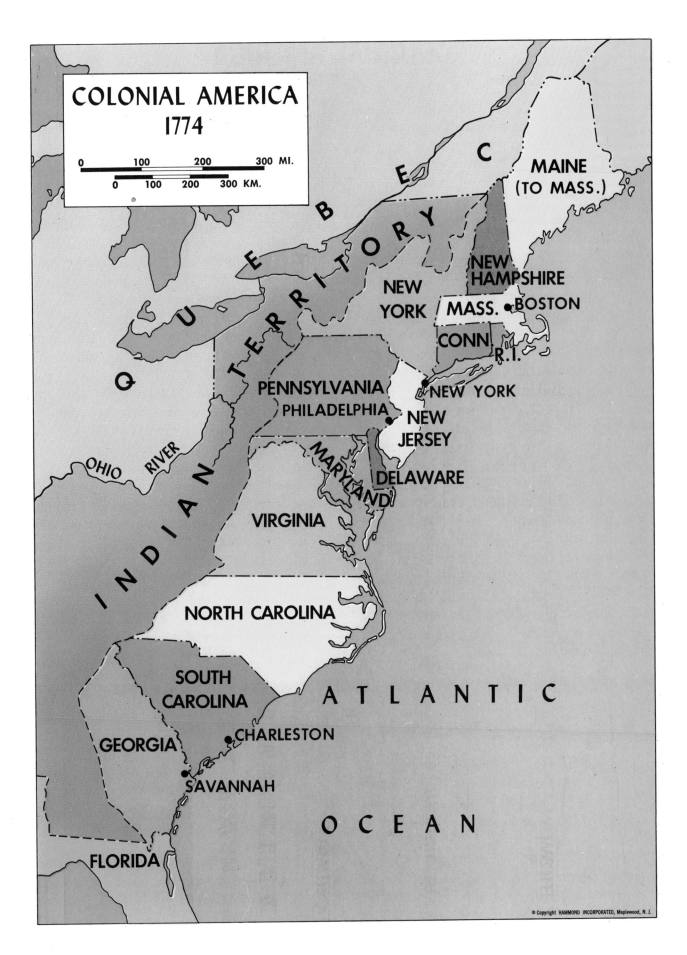

COLONIAL AMERICA 1774

0   100   200   300 MI.

0   100   200   300 KM.

Q U E B E C

MAINE (TO MASS.)

I N D I A N   T E R R I T O R Y

NEW HAMPSHIRE

NEW YORK

MASS.   •BOSTON

CONN

R.I.

PENNSYLVANIA

NEW YORK

PHILADELPHIA   NEW JERSEY

OHIO   RIVER

MARYLAND

DELAWARE

VIRGINIA

NORTH CAROLINA

SOUTH CAROLINA

A T L A N T I C

GEORGIA   •CHARLESTON

•SAVANNAH

FLORIDA

O C E A N

COLONIAL AMERICA
MAP—PAGE 13

By the time the French and Indian War had ended, the British colonists had begun to think of themselves as being more American than British. They looked with pride at the 13 colonies they had established — Virginia, Massachusetts (which included Maine), Rhode Island, New Hampshire, Connecticut, Delaware, Maryland, New York, New Jersey, North Carolina, South Carolina, Pennsylvania, and Georgia. To the south of the colonies was the Spanish colony of Florida.

In general, the colonies were prosperous. In the Northeast, small farms dotted the landscape. Small shipbuilding and textile industries were developing there. Shipping and trading were becoming more important. One of the cities that profited from the growth of shipping and trade was Boston. Its harbor was filled with ships from other nations and other colonies.

The people of the Northeast were fiercely democratic. They ran their local government through town meetings. In these meetings, landowners discussed their communities' problems and voted on how to deal with them.

To the south, the Middle Colonies were also growing rapidly. Here, too, agriculture flourished, as did shipping and trading. As centers of commerce, New York and Philadelphia became important cities.

In the South, an economy based on agriculture and trade was also developing. There, large plantations and smaller farms produced great amounts of tobacco and cotton for use in the colonies and abroad. The cities of Charleston and Savannah were soon busy ports from which the goods of the South went out daily.

The population of the 13 British colonies stood at two million. The colonial ways began to differ from ways in Europe. The colonists had many new experiences. They lived under different conditions. As a result, many customs and attitudes began to change. The colonists felt strongly that America was theirs. They wanted to run it themselves, with little interference from people across the ocean.

The government in Great Britain, however, had a different idea. It looked on the colonies as theirs. It believed it had the right to tax the colonists and make laws for them. The British government also thought that the colonies should help pay for the French and Indian War — the war that had cleared the French from the Ohio Valley.

Trouble between the independent-minded Americans and the government in Britain grew. The disagreement over who had the right to rule would eventually lead to the American Revolution.

---

1. Boston, New York, Philadelphia, Charleston, and Savannah became important shipping centers. Construct a chart which lists each of these cities and the area in which each city is located (Northeast, Middle, South). Then add to your chart those products which were shipped from each city.

2. Do you feel that those colonies which bordered on the Indian Territory and Quebec encountered any problems different from those faced by other colonies? Explain your answer in at least one or two paragraphs.

3. Imagine that you're a colonist in one of the three major areas (Northeast, Middle, South). Write a short essay on your lifestyle including social, governmental, and business factors. Consult an encyclopedia if you wish.

4. If you were a member of the British government, how would you view the colonies across the ocean? Explain as fully as possible.

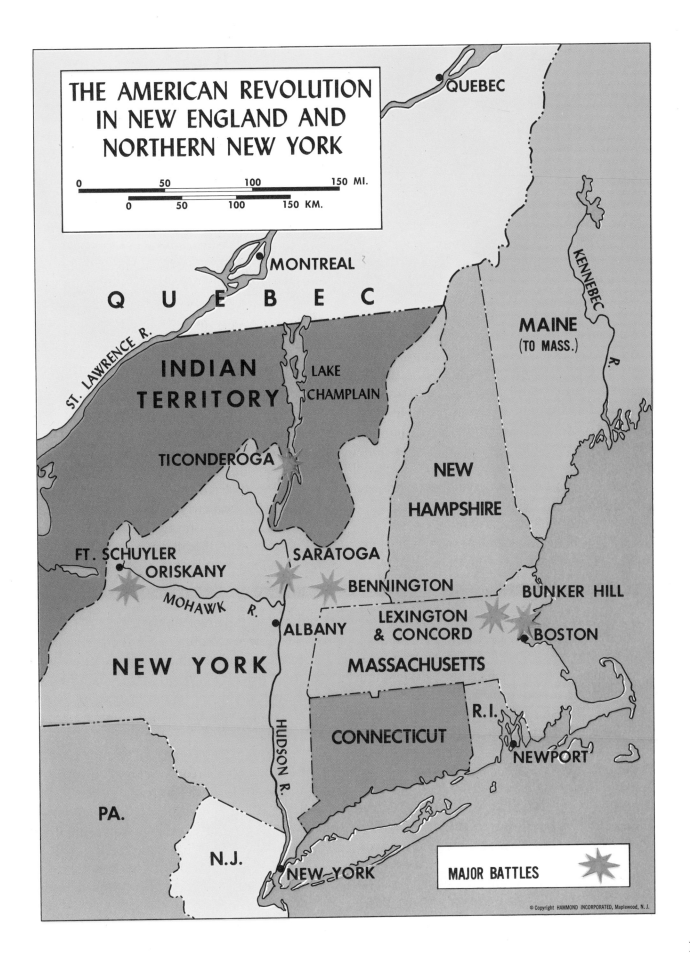

THE AMERICAN REVOLUTION IN NEW ENGLAND AND NORTHERN NEW YORK

0   50   100   150 MI.

0   50   100   150 KM.

QUEBEC

MONTREAL

Q U E B E C

ST. LAWRENCE R.

INDIAN TERRITORY

LAKE CHAMPLAIN

MAINE (TO MASS.)

KENNEBEC R.

TICONDEROGA

NEW HAMPSHIRE

FT. SCHUYLER
ORISKANY

SARATOGA

BENNINGTON

BUNKER HILL

MOHAWK R.

LEXINGTON & CONCORD

BOSTON

ALBANY

MASSACHUSETTS

NEW YORK

R.I.

CONNECTICUT

HUDSON R.

NEWPORT

PA.

N.J.

NEW YORK

MAJOR BATTLES

© Copyright HAMMOND INCORPORATED, Maplewood, N. J.

15

THE AMERICAN REVOLUTION

MAPS—PAGES 15, 17, 18

The friction between the colonists and the British finally led to war in 1775. The colonists had been training soldiers and storing weapons for them. The British learned that the colonists had a storehouse in Concord, Massachusetts, and they sent their redcoats to capture it. Colonial soldiers decided it was time to resist, and they attacked the British soldiers at Lexington. The American Revolution had begun. It would continue for the next six and a half years.

At first look, it seemed that the colonists were doomed to lose. Their enemy was a powerful European nation. The English had been at war almost constantly for the past 100 years. Its army and navy were well trained, well disciplined, and well equipped. Its commanders were battle veterans. The colonists, on the other hand, were not professional soldiers. They were not well equipped or well trained for battle. Nor were they organized into a tightly knit fighting force.

But on second look, the fight was not so one-sided. The British had disadvantages too. For one thing, they were not fighting on familiar home ground, as the colonists were. For another, the colonies covered a vast area (about 1,000 by 600 miles or 1,600 by 1,000 kilometers). Even if the British won battles and captured land, they would not be able to spare the thousands of troops needed to hold onto it. Finally, British troops would be thousands of miles away from their source of supply, Great Britain.

Over the years that followed, the colonists made the most of these British disadvantages. They lost many battles to their enemy; but as the American general Nathanael Greene said, "We fight, get beat, rise, and fight again."

Eventually, the colonists' persistence wore the enemy down. The British back home grew tired of the long and expensive war. When they learned of a surprise victory of the Americans at Yorktown in Virginia in October 1781, they decided it was all over. Two years later, a peace treaty was signed between Great Britain and the newly formed United States of America. Great Britain gave the United States all of its land west to the Mississippi River and north to the Great Lakes.

1. On a sheet of tracing paper, trace any *one* of the maps on pages 15, 17, or 18. Indicate the major battles of that particular region with either a blue star, designating American victory or with a red star, designating British victory. Be sure to include the date of each conflict as well. You may consult an encyclopedia to assist you in obtaining the data for this question.

2. Most battles in New England took place between 1775 and 1777. Most battles in the Middle Colonies took place between 1776 and 1778. The battles in the South took place between 1778 and 1781. Why do you think the battle area moved from north to south? Explain your answer in one paragraph.

3. Look at the maps on pages 15, 17, and 18. Then, in one column, list the major inland battles and the other major battles which took place in seaports. Do you think the British preferred inland or seaport battles? Explain your answer in two or more paragraphs.

4. Write two paragraphs which compare the advantages and disadvantages of the British forces with those of the American troops.

5. Using the scale on page 15, determine the longest distance between battle sites shown on this map. Do the same for the maps on pages 17 and 18 making sure you use only the scale which accompanies each map, since they do differ in each case. Record your findings on a separate sheet of paper.

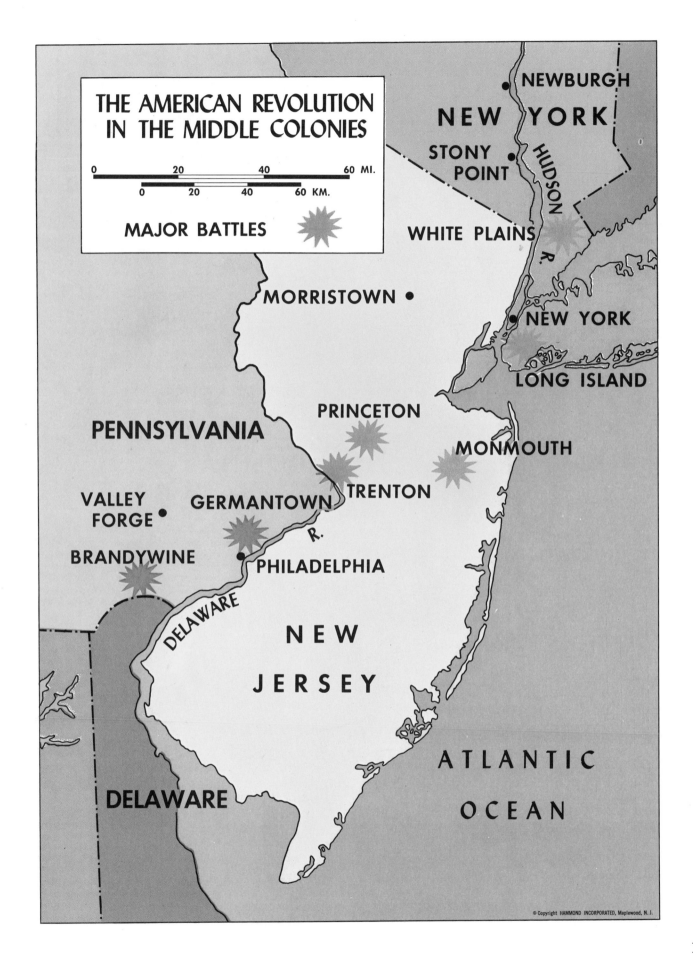

THE AMERICAN REVOLUTION
IN THE MIDDLE COLONIES

0   20   40   60 MI.

0   20   40   60 KM.

MAJOR BATTLES

NEWBURGH

NEW YORK

STONY
POINT

HUDSON R.

WHITE PLAINS

MORRISTOWN

NEW YORK

LONG ISLAND

PRINCETON

PENNSYLVANIA

MONMOUTH

VALLEY
FORGE

GERMANTOWN

TRENTON

BRANDYWINE

DELAWARE R.

PHILADELPHIA

NEW

JERSEY

DELAWARE

ATLANTIC

OCEAN

© Copyright HAMMOND INCORPORATED, Maplewood, N.J.

17

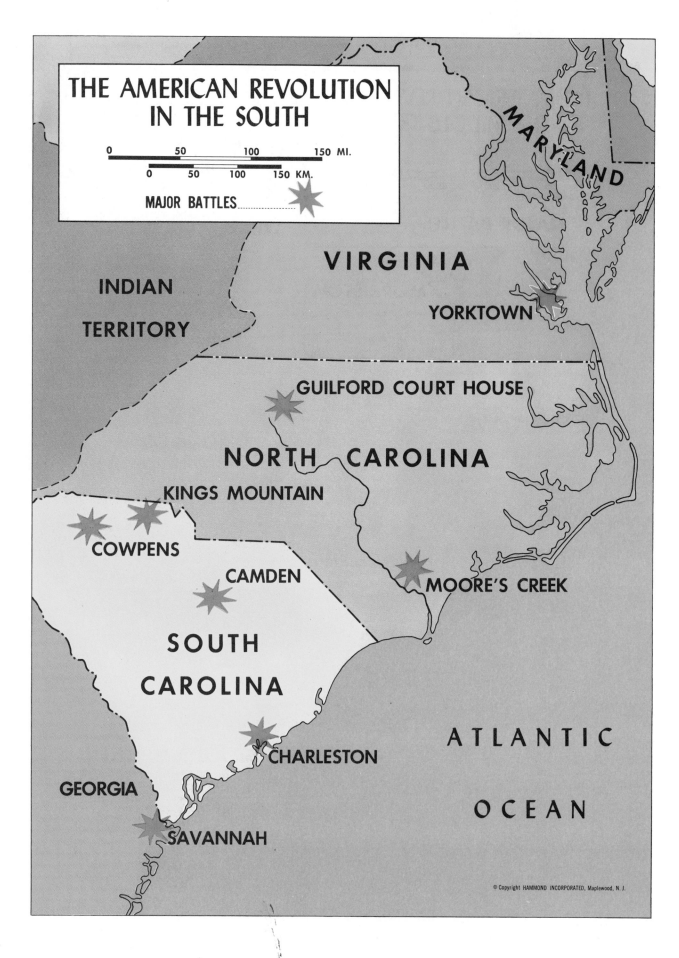

THE AMERICAN REVOLUTION
IN THE SOUTH

0   50   100   150 MI.
0   50   100   150 KM.

MAJOR BATTLES

MARYLAND

VIRGINIA

INDIAN TERRITORY

YORKTOWN

GUILFORD COURT HOUSE

NORTH CAROLINA

KINGS MOUNTAIN

COWPENS

CAMDEN

MOORE'S CREEK

SOUTH CAROLINA

CHARLESTON

GEORGIA

ATLANTIC

OCEAN

SAVANNAH

© Copyright HAMMOND INCORPORATED, Maplewood, N. J.

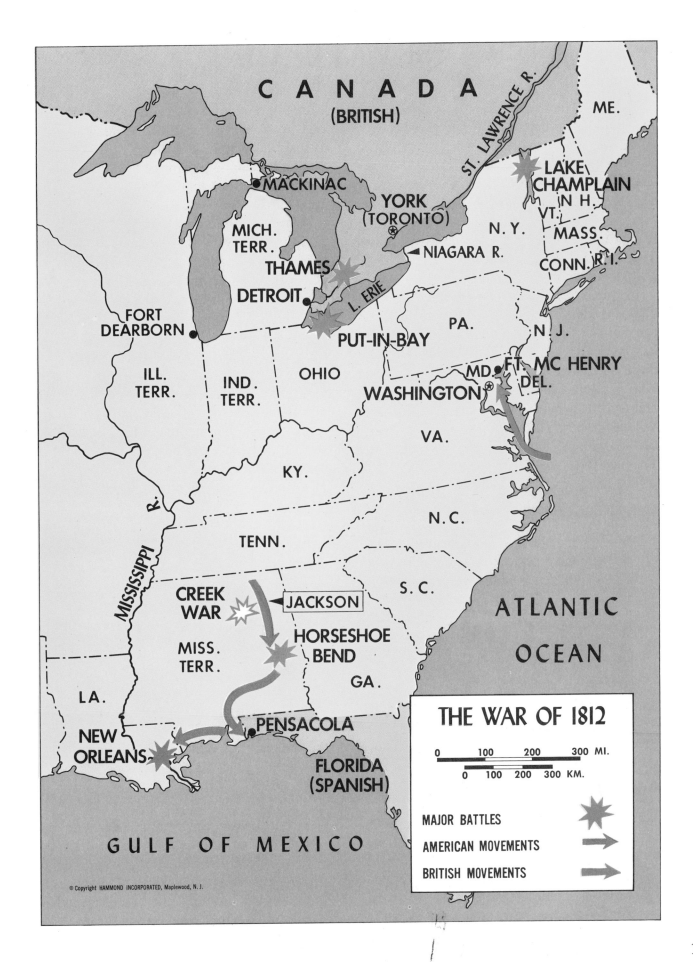

CANADA
(BRITISH)

ME.

ST. LAWRENCE R.

MACKINAC

YORK
(TORONTO)

LAKE
CHAMPLAIN
N.H.

VT.

N.Y.

MASS.

MICH.
TERR.

NIAGARA R.

CONN. R.I.

THAMES

DETROIT

L. ERIE

PA.

N.J.

FORT
DEARBORN

PUT-IN-BAY

FT. MC HENRY

MD.

DEL.

ILL.
TERR.

IND.
TERR.

OHIO

WASHINGTON

VA.

KY.

N.C.

TENN.

MISSISSIPPI R.

S.C.

CREEK
WAR

JACKSON

ATLANTIC

OCEAN

MISS.
TERR.

HORSESHOE
BEND

GA.

LA.

THE WAR OF 1812

PENSACOLA

0   100   200   300 MI.

NEW
ORLEANS

0   100   200   300 KM.

FLORIDA
(SPANISH)

MAJOR BATTLES

GULF OF MEXICO

AMERICAN MOVEMENTS

BRITISH MOVEMENTS

© Copyright HAMMOND INCORPORATED, Maplewood, N.J.

THE WAR OF 1812
MAP—PAGE 19

Trouble soon again arose between the British and Americans. It began when the British interfered with the American right to freedom of the seas. The British were trying to stop United States trade with other nations by seizing American ships. Worse than that, they were seizing American seamen and forcing, or impressing, them into the British navy. The British claimed that the seamen were British and deserters from their navy.

In June 1812, Congress declared war on Great Britain. Early battles were disastrous for the Americans because of the small size of its navy. But in 1813, the Americans were more successful. In a naval battle on Lake Erie, Captain Oliver Perry defeated the British and forced them to abandon Detroit. General William Henry Harrison pursued the fleeing British troops and defeated them at the Thames River.

The next year the British planned three campaigns against the Americans. The first one took place on Lake Champlain. The British fleet that had been sent there was beaten by Captain Thomas Macdonough.

In the second campaign, an invading force sailed up the Potomac River toward the capital at Washington, D.C. They set fire to the city, and then made for Baltimore. Here they were stopped by American troops at Fort McHenry. It was this battle that inspired Francis Scott Key to write "The Star-Spangled Banner."

The third campaign was launched against New Orleans in 1815. General Andrew Jackson's troops, fresh from fighting against the Indians in the Mississippi Territory, soon defeated the British. Actually, this final battle was fought two weeks after the war had officially ended. Neither the Americans nor the British knew that a peace treaty had been signed in Belgium, Europe, on Christmas Eve, 1814.

1. Examine the battle sites on the map on page 19. Why do you think that the majority of battles took place near water? Explain.

2. Write a paragraph or two in which you outline the reasons that prompted Americans to declare war on the British.

SETTLEMENT OF THE UNITED STATES

The United States has had many frontiers during its development. There always seemed to be more untouched land to the west. And there were always people who wanted to move deep into that wilderness. As soon as one area was settled, they moved on to the next. Nothing stopped them — neither mountains, forests, nor vast treeless plains. Life was hard for the settlers. Yet with hard work and courage, they built up the West.

1. The movement west seemed to progress in stages. Compare the map on page 21 and the map of the United States on the inside front cover. List on a sheet of paper the geographical features (mountains or rivers) which stalled movement at each stage.

2. Imagine that you're a settler moving west.

In one or two paragraphs, describe the dangers and hardships you would expect to face as you progressed on your journey. Include why you chose to face difficult odds despite discouraging reports you had received from those who set out before you.

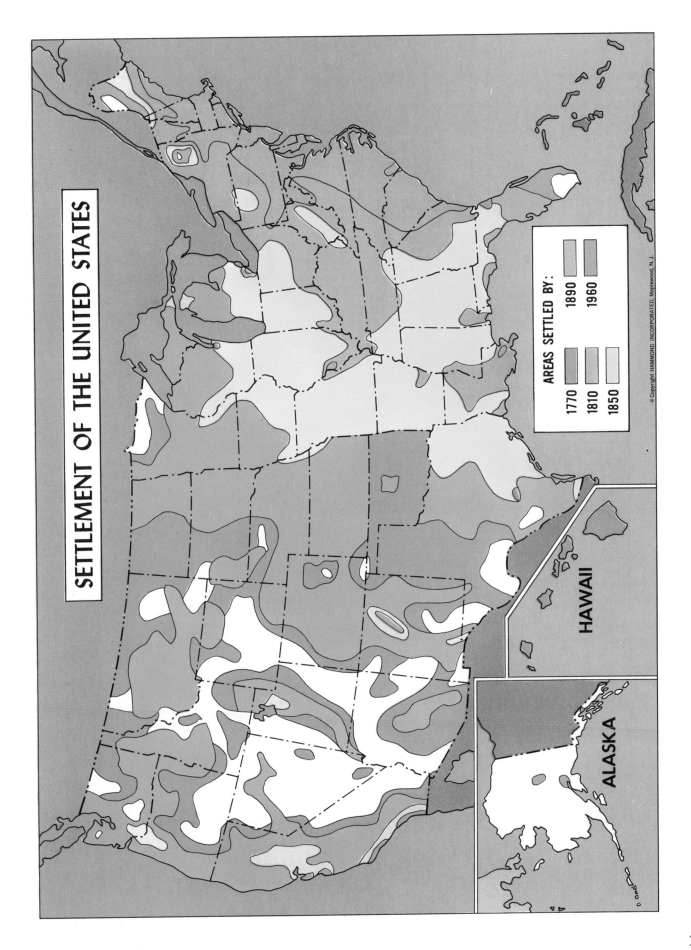

SETTLEMENT OF THE UNITED STATES

AREAS SETTLED BY:

1770	1890
1810	1960
1850	

© Copyright HAMMOND INCORPORATED, Maplewood, N.J.

HAWAII

ALASKA

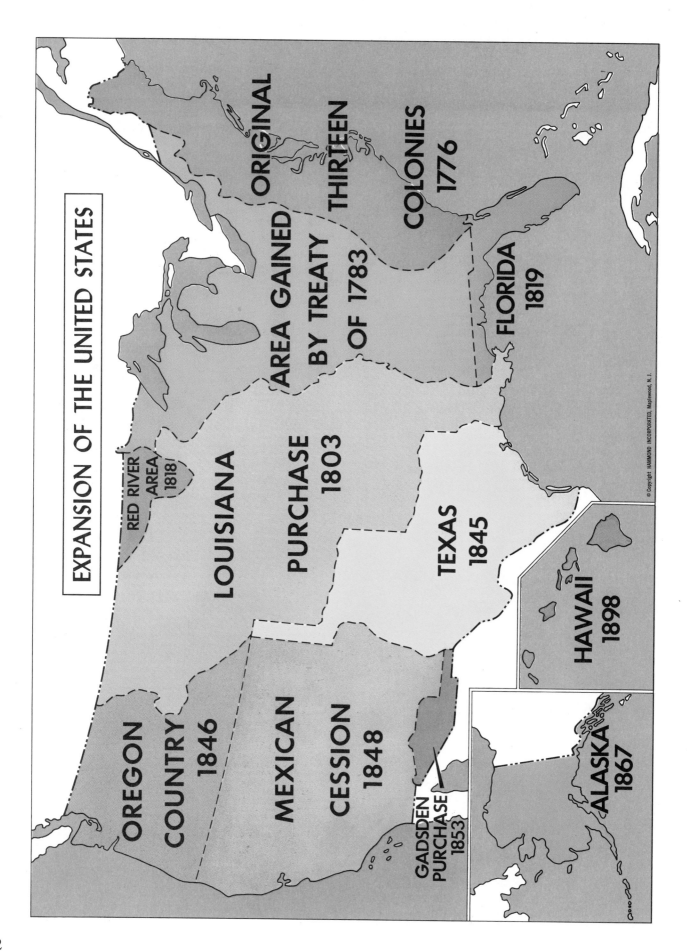

EXPANSION OF THE UNITED STATES

ORIGINAL THIRTEEN COLONIES 1776

AREA GAINED BY TREATY OF 1783

FLORIDA 1819

RED RIVER AREA 1818

LOUISIANA PURCHASE 1803

TEXAS 1845

HAWAII 1898

OREGON COUNTRY 1846

MEXICAN CESSION 1848

GADSDEN PURCHASE 1853

ALASKA 1867

© Copyright HAMMOND INCORPORATED, Maplewood, N. J.

22

EXPANSION OF THE UNITED STATES

The expansion of the United States from the Atlantic Ocean to the Pacific resulted from war, treaty, and purchase.

The American Revolution won for the new nation its first big piece of land. The British agreed to let the Americans have all the territory from the boundary of the original colonies to the Mississippi River.

A great land bargain brought the next big parcel of territory to the Americans. France under the ruler Napoleon owned the immense Louisiana Territory. Napoleon's wars in Europe were costing vast amounts of money. So the French offered the territory for sale. Thomas Jefferson, as President of the United States, offered France $15 million for it. The French accepted this offer, which amounted to two or three cents an acre. With this purchase, the United States doubled its size.

North of the Louisiana Territory was a piece of land that both Britain and the United States claimed. In 1818, they agreed that it should be American land.

At this same time, the United States was also having a dispute over land with Spain. The land in question was Florida. At first the United States simply took over the western part of Florida. Then General Andrew Jackson and his troops invaded the eastern part. In 1819, the Americans and the Spaniards met and decided on a treaty. Spain agreed to give up all claim to land east of the Mississippi River. Florida became part of the United States.

Spain continued to control vast areas of land west of the Mississippi. It claimed the entire Southwest. But in 1821, Spain's hold was broken. Mexico declared itself a separate nation and claimed the Southwest as its own. American settlers poured into this Mexican territory, especially into Texas. By the 1830s, they were fighting the Mexicans to make Texas independent. Texas succeeded, and in 1845 it became part of the United States.

In 1846, the United States went to war with Mexico. Two years later, the Mexicans ceded a vast area extending to the Pacific Ocean to the Americans for $15 million. Then the American government told its minister to Mexico, James Gadsden, to buy one final piece of land from Mexico for $10 million. The entire Southwest was now in the hands of Americans.

To the north, the British and Americans had had a dispute over who owned the Oregon Country. In the same year that the Mexican War began, Britain and the United States settled their dispute by treaty. The Oregon Country was now an American outpost. And, west of the Great Lakes, the northern boundary of the United States ran along the 49th parallel all the way to the Pacific coast.

In 1867, the United States purchased Alaska from the Russians for a little more than $7 million. In 1898, the nation took over Hawaii at the request of American settlers there. The United States had expanded into all of what would be its 50 states.

---

1. On a sheet of tracing paper, trace the map on page 22 and include all boundaries of land added to the United States. Label each, and name the nation the United States dealt with in gaining the land.
2. Compare the map on page 22 and the map of the United States on the inside front cover. What geographical feature was the western boundary for the Original Thirteen Colonies, the area gained by the Treaty of 1783, the southwest boundary of Texas, and the northern boundary of the Gadsden Purchase? Answer on a sheet of paper.

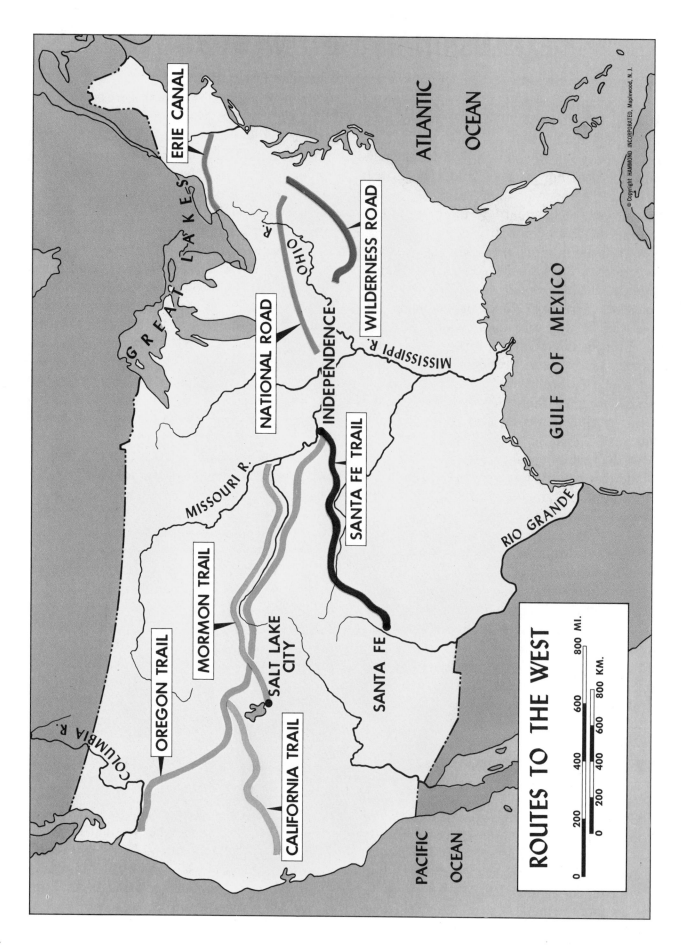

ATLANTIC OCEAN

GULF OF MEXICO

PACIFIC OCEAN

GREAT LAKES

ERIE CANAL

WILDERNESS ROAD

NATIONAL ROAD

INDEPENDENCE

SANTA FE TRAIL

OHIO R.

MISSISSIPPI R.

MISSOURI R.

RIO GRANDE

COLUMBIA R.

OREGON TRAIL

MORMON TRAIL

SALT LAKE CITY

CALIFORNIA TRAIL

SANTA FE

ROUTES TO THE WEST

| 0 | 200 | 400 | 600 | 800 MI. |

| 0 | 200 | 400 | 600 | 800 KM. |

© Copyright HAMMOND INCORPORATED, Maplewood, N.J.

24

ROUTES TO THE WEST

Although many people wanted to go west in America, the road there was a difficult one. At first, the Appalachian Mountains blocked the way. But in 1775, the great woodsman and explorer Daniel Boone carved a path through the Appalachians. He found "a door through the mountain wall" called the Cumberland Gap. His Wilderness Road went through this gap and into the rich farming and hunting lands of Kentucky and beyond.

Congress also came to the aid of those who wanted to settle in the West. In 1811, the government agreed to finance the National Road, also called the Cumberland Road. Originally, this road extended from Maryland as far west as the city of Wheeling. But in a few years, it had extended nearly to the Mississippi River.

Still another route into this area of the United States was the Ohio River. Settlers sailed down it on flatboats into the rich Ohio Valley.

The Erie Canal, begun in 1817, provided another way of moving people and goods to the west and back again. For eight years, immigrant laborers struggled to dig its nearly 400 miles (644 kilometers) of waterway, joining the Hudson River with Lake Erie. When their work was completed, inexpensive travel and shipping from the east coast to the Great Lakes were a reality.

All of these routes made it easier for settlers to reach the area east of the Mississippi River. But the area west of the Mississippi was much larger and travel across it was more difficult.

The settlers had to follow the trails that fur trappers and traders had blazed. These trails usually began at the Missouri River and were a mixture of overland and water routes. Sometimes settlers traveled alongside rivers in wagons. Sometimes they turned their wagons into boats. They found ways to cross mountains and deserts.

Settlers who wanted to go to the Southwest followed the Santa Fe Trail. It had been opened in the 1820s by traders who exchanged manufactured goods for Mexican silver and gold.

The Oregon Trail served those pioneers who had caught "Oregon fever" and wanted farmland out there. Fur trappers who had first come west along this trail led the wagon trains of settlers along it. By the 1840s, a thousand people a year were entering Oregon Country.

By 1849, people were traveling the Oregon Trail who were not bound for farms in the Northwest. Instead they were branching off onto the California Trail. They were the "Forty-Niners"— seekers after the gold that had been discovered in California in 1848.

And then there was the Mormon Trail. The people who first traveled this road were not seeking gold. Nor were they seeking only farmland. They were members of a religious group that had been forced out of settlements in the east. The Mormons wanted a place where they could practice their religion freely, as they wished. They found it when they reached the Great Salt Lake in what is now Utah.

---

1. Look at page 24 and write answers to the following questions: What body of water seemed to be important to the development of several routes west? How many routes did this body of water affect? Name them. Which main direction did each follow?
2. In one or two paragraphs, discuss the advantages and disadvantages of following a land route as opposed to following a water route in the journey west.
3. Read about the Gold Rush of 1849 in an encyclopedia. Then write two paragraphs telling why you think/don't think you would have caught "gold fever."

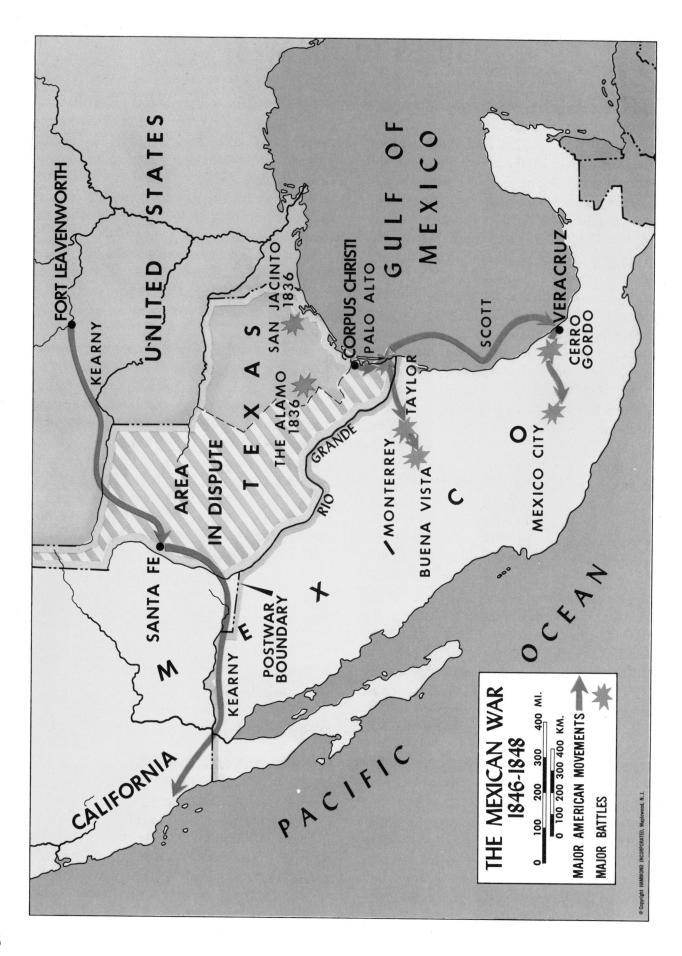

UNITED STATES

FORT LEAVENWORTH

KEARNY

TEXAS

SAN JACINTO 1836

THE ALAMO 1836

AREA IN DISPUTE

SANTA FE

M

KEARNY

POSTWAR BOUNDARY

E

X

RIO GRANDE

CALIFORNIA

CORPUS CHRISTI
PALO ALTO

GULF OF MEXICO

MONTERREY

TAYLOR

BUENA VISTA

C

O

MEXICO CITY

SCOTT

VERACRUZ

CERRO GORDO

PACIFIC OCEAN

THE MEXICAN WAR
1846-1848

100   200   300   400 MI.

0 100 200 300 400 KM.

0

MAJOR AMERICAN MOVEMENTS

MAJOR BATTLES

© Copyright HAMMOND INCORPORATED, Maplewood, N.J.

THE MEXICAN WAR

It is true that Texas fought for its independence from Mexico in such famous battles as those at The Alamo and at San Jacinto. And it is true that Texas became a state in 1845. But it is not true that Mexico accepted the situation completely. The Mexicans did not agree that the United States owned all of the land it claimed as part of Texas in 1845. The ownership of all of western Texas was in question.

Friction over this dispute and over money Americans said Mexico owed them led the two nations to war in 1846.

The United States attacked Mexico in three places. First, Colonel Stephen Kearny and his troops were sent from Fort Leavenworth, Kansas, through the Southwest to California. Second, General Zachary Taylor and his army marched from Corpus Christi, Texas, across the disputed area and into Mexico. Third, General Winfield Scott and his soldiers invaded southern Mexico and marched inland to the capital, Mexico City.

1. On a separate sheet of paper, write a paragraph explaining the causes of the dispute between the United States and Mexico.
2. Refer to page 26. Then make a chart in which you include the following information: the leaders of the three American invasions, the directions which each followed, whether land or water routes were taken, and the major battles in which the leaders fought.

FREE AND SLAVE STATES IN 1854

MAP—PAGE 28

One of the worst disputes in American history raged over slavery. Many people in the South felt that they had to have their slaves to produce their main crop — cotton. They also believed that slaves were treated as well as factory workers in the North. Many people in the North took an opposite view. They thought that slavery was inhuman and had no place in a democratic country.

For many years, the nation was able to keep a balance between North and South. The states were fairly evenly divided between those that had slavery and those that did not. Each time a slave state would enter the Union, so would a free state.

But in 1854, that balance seemed to be upset. Congress created two new territories, Kansas and Nebraska. Both were open to slavery. That meant that the territories would decide the slavery question themselves. If the territories came into the Union as slave states, the South would be more powerful than the North.

Tension between the North and South grew.

1. Why did the people of the South feel that they needed slaves? Why did the people of the North disagree? On a separate sheet of paper, explain your answer in one paragraph.
2. Refer to the map on page 28. Divide your paper into two columns. On the left side, list the slave states and territories and on the right, list the free states and territories.
3. If the open territories all chose slavery, would the slave or free states have the advantage in the slavery dispute?
4. Which free state extended the farthest south? Which slave state extended the farthest north? Write your answers on a sheet of paper.

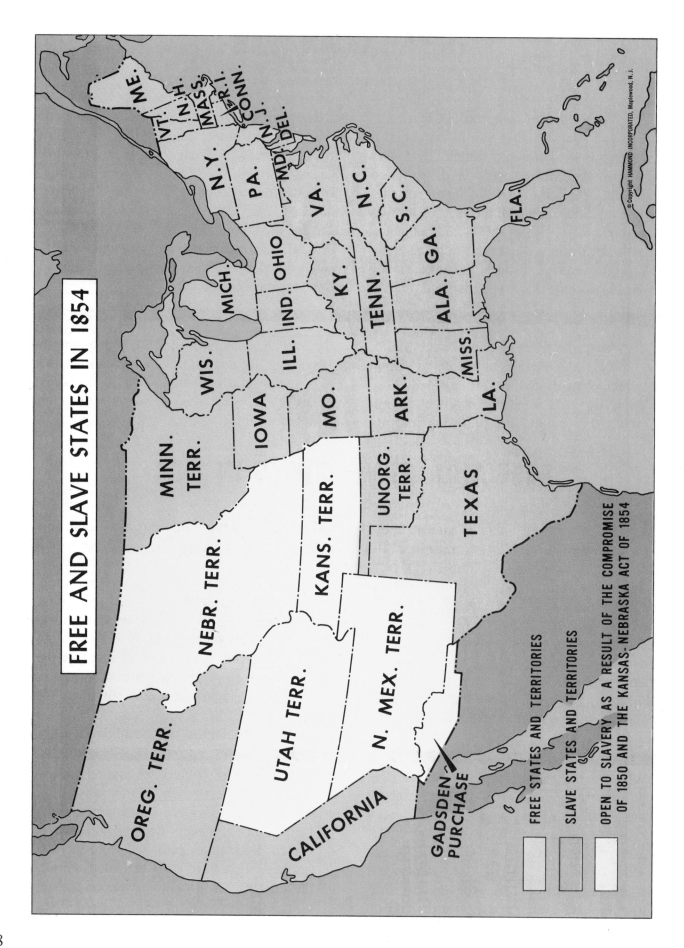

FREE AND SLAVE STATES IN 1854

ME.
VT.
N.H.
MASS.
R.I.
CONN.
N.Y.
N.J.
PA.
MD.
DEL.
OHIO
VA.
N.C.
S.C.
FLA.
MICH.
IND.
KY.
TENN.
ALA.
GA.
WIS.
ILL.
MISS.
IOWA
MO.
ARK.
LA.
MINN. TERR.
NEBR. TERR.
KANS. TERR.
UNORG. TERR.
TEXAS
OREG. TERR.
UTAH TERR.
N. MEX. TERR.
CALIFORNIA
GADSDEN PURCHASE

FREE STATES AND TERRITORIES

SLAVE STATES AND TERRITORIES

OPEN TO SLAVERY AS A RESULT OF THE COMPROMISE
OF 1850 AND THE KANSAS-NEBRASKA ACT OF 1854

© Copyright HAMMOND INCORPORATED, Maplewood, N.J.

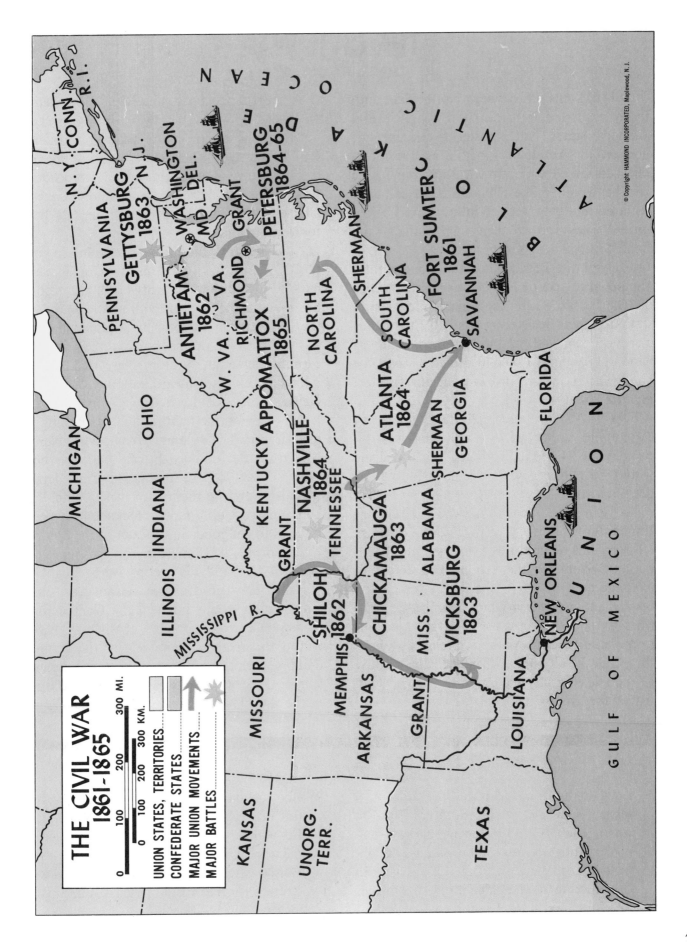

THE CIVIL WAR 1861-1865

UNION STATES, TERRITORIES
CONFEDERATE STATES
MAJOR UNION MOVEMENTS
MAJOR BATTLES

0   100   200   300 MI.

0   100   200   300 KM.

PENNSYLVANIA
GETTYSBURG 1863
N.Y.   CONN.   R.I.
N.J.
WASHINGTON
MD.   DEL.
ANTIETAM 1862
W. VA.   VA.
RICHMOND
GRANT
APPOMATTOX 1865
PETERSBURG 1864-65
NORTH CAROLINA
SHERMAN
SOUTH CAROLINA
FORT SUMTER 1861
SAVANNAH

MICHIGAN
OHIO
INDIANA
ILLINOIS
KENTUCKY
NASHVILLE 1864
GRANT
TENNESSEE
CHICKAMAUGA 1863
ATLANTA 1864
SHERMAN
GEORGIA
FLORIDA

MISSISSIPPI R.
SHILOH 1862
MEMPHIS
MISS.   ALABAMA
VICKSBURG 1863

MISSOURI
ARKANSAS
GRANT
LOUISIANA
NEW ORLEANS

KANSAS
UNORG. TERR.
TEXAS

GULF OF MEXICO

ATLANTIC OCEAN

BLOCKADE

U N I O N

© Copyright HAMMOND INCORPORATED, Maplewood, N. J.

29

THE CIVIL WAR

MAPS—PAGES 29, 31

In 1861, tensions between North and South finally exploded into the Civil War. Several southern states had refused to accept the election of Abraham Lincoln as President. They disagreed violently with the changes he said he would make. Therefore, these states declared that they were no longer a part of the Union. They formed their own union — the Confederate States of America.

The fighting began when the Confederates attempted to occupy Fort Sumter in the harbor of Charleston, South Carolina. Union forces stationed there resisted at first. But then they marched out and left the fort in southern hands. President Lincoln declared that the Union faced an armed revolt and that it must fight to defeat the rebels.

The Union plan was to split the Confederacy by gaining control of the western rivers, especially the Mississippi. Control of these rivers would open the way for the invasion of the deep South.

Early in 1862, General Ulysses S. Grant left Illinois with his troops and proceeded south. His victories secured the Tennessee and Cumberland rivers for the Union. The defeat of Confederate forces in the battle of Shiloh opened the way for a Union march down the Mississippi. By May 1863, Grant and his troops had reached Vicksburg. For six weeks they kept the city under siege. Finally, on July 4, the starving city gave up. The North controlled the Mississippi.

A short while later, another Union victory weakened the South. Union forces overran Chattanooga, an important rail center in southern Tennessee. When Union troops pursued the retreating Confederates, they were not so lucky. The southerners stood and fought at Chickamauga and beat the northerners back to Chattanooga.

Nevertheless, Union forces were still in good position. In 1864, General William T. Sherman left Chattanooga with 100,000 troops. From there they began a dramatic march to the sea. After first capturing Atlanta, they cut a wide path of destruction on their way to capture Savannah. Victory there freed Union troops to move northward and hit Confederate General Robert E. Lee's troops from behind.

All of this time, fighting had been going on in Virginia, Maryland, and Pennsylvania. Bloody battle followed bloody battle as both sides suffered terrible losses. The Confederacy was also suffering the loss of its shipping. The Union had set up a naval blockade to make it difficult to get goods into or out of the South.

By spring of 1865, the end was in sight. General Lee and his troops were caught in Virginia between Generals Grant and Sherman. Union troops pursued the Confederates to Appomattox Court House, where Lee was forced to surrender. The rest of the Confederate generals surrendered in the following weeks. Over 600,000 men had died by the end of the war. The South was severely hurt.

1. Look at the map on page 29. Then on a separate sheet of paper, name the state in which each of the following battles took place: Antietam, Nashville, Atlanta, Shiloh, Gettysburg. Which of these places were in Confederate states? Which of these places were in Union states?

2. Look at page 31. Did the majority of battles take place in the North or the South? Do you think this affected the outcome of the war? Explain your answer.

3. Why was setting up a naval blockade a wise strategy for the North? Discuss your answer in a paragraph.

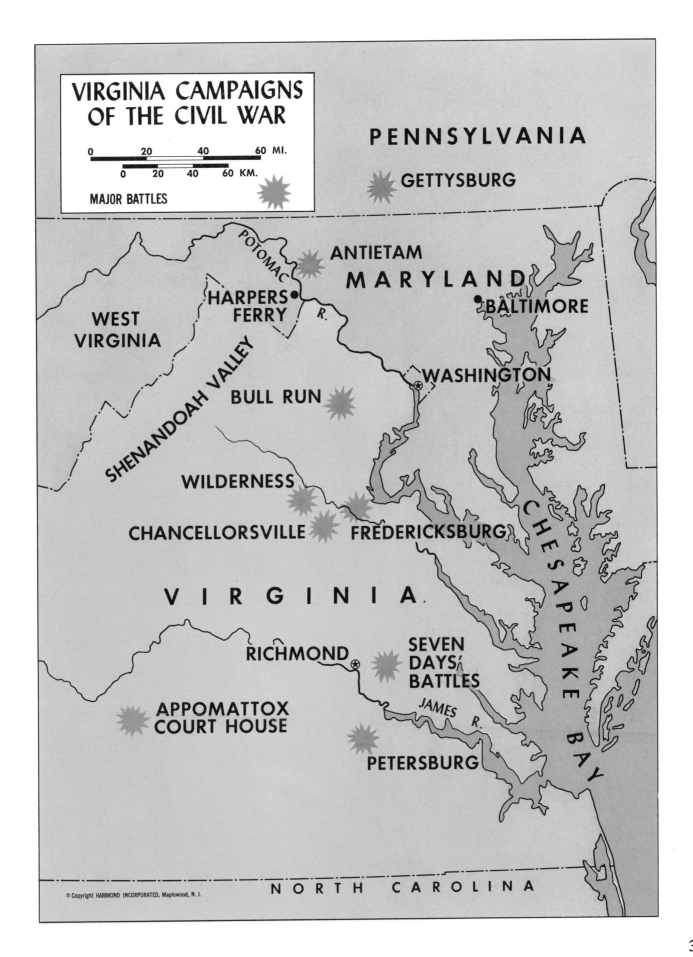

VIRGINIA CAMPAIGNS OF THE CIVIL WAR

0   20   40   60 MI.

0   20   40   60 KM.

MAJOR BATTLES

PENNSYLVANIA

GETTYSBURG

POTOMAC

ANTIETAM

MARYLAND

HARPERS FERRY

R.

BALTIMORE

WEST VIRGINIA

WASHINGTON

SHENANDOAH VALLEY

BULL RUN

WILDERNESS

CHANCELLORSVILLE   FREDERICKSBURG

CHESAPEAKE BAY

V I R G I N I A

RICHMOND

SEVEN DAYS' BATTLES

APPOMATTOX COURT HOUSE

JAMES   R.

PETERSBURG

© Copyright HAMMOND INCORPORATED, Maplewood, N. J.

N O R T H   C A R O L I N A

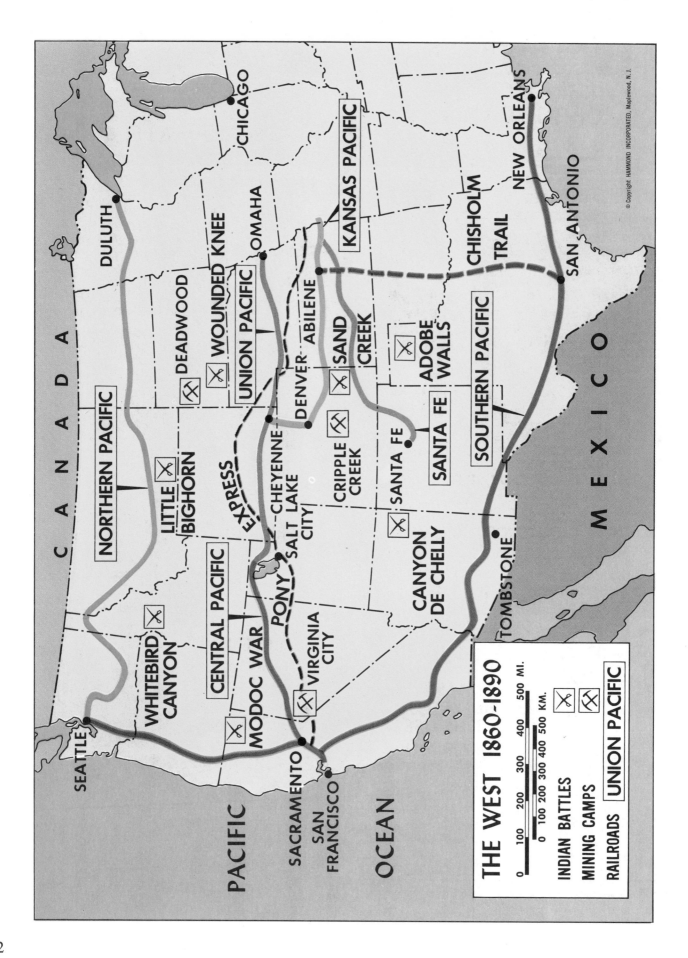

THE WEST 1860-1890

CANADA

MEXICO

PACIFIC OCEAN

Cities and places:
CHICAGO
DULUTH
NEW ORLEANS
SAN ANTONIO
OMAHA
DEADWOOD
WOUNDED KNEE
ABILENE
DENVER
SAND CREEK
ADOBE WALLS
SANTA FE
CHEYENNE
CRIPPLE CREEK
SALT LAKE CITY
CANYON DE CHELLY
TOMBSTONE
VIRGINIA CITY
WHITEBIRD CANYON
SEATTLE
SACRAMENTO
SAN FRANCISCO

Railroads and trails:
KANSAS PACIFIC
CHISHOLM TRAIL
UNION PACIFIC
SOUTHERN PACIFIC
NORTHERN PACIFIC
SANTA FE
LITTLE BIGHORN
EXPRESS
CENTRAL PACIFIC
PONY
MODOC WAR

Legend:

INDIAN BATTLES	
MINING CAMPS	
RAILROADS	UNION PACIFIC

100 0 100 200 300 400 500 MI.

100 0 100 200 300 400 500 KM.

© Copyright HAMMOND INCORPORATED, Maplewood, N.J.

32

THE WEST 1860-1890

Four kinds of activity gave the West its distinctive character as it developed. These included Indian fighting, mining, railroad building, and cattle raising.

It is not surprising that the Indians, who wanted to keep what they had, clashed with the newcomers who tried to take it from them. As settlers poured into the West, claiming more and more land, the Indians fought back. The government in Washington, D.C., in turn, sent the army to protect the settlers. The battles and massacres that followed are tragic chapters in the history of the West.

Several of the clashes between the Indians and the American cavalry have become famous. The massacre that occurred in 1864 at Sand Creek is one example. It was here that soldiers attacked the winter camp of a band of peaceful Cheyenne and killed hundreds of them. This caused the plains wars to spread.

The battle at Little Big Horn, called "Custer's Last Stand," took place in 1876. A large force of Sioux and Cheyenne met General George Armstrong Custer's Seventh Cavalry and wiped out 231 men. This shocked the nation and the government sent more troops to the West. In 1890, the Seventh Cavalry wiped out a band of Sioux at Wounded Knee, South Dakota. This battle marked the end of the Indian wars.

Part of what had angered the Indians in the first place were the miners. The Indians had watched thousands of people pour into Virginia City in 1859 to mine the Comstock Lode — the richest gold and silver find ever. In 1875, another rich strike was made in the Black Hills of the Dakota Territory. This was sacred land to the Indians, but the miners came anyway. The result was the battle at Little Big Horn.

The Indians were also angry about the coming of the train crews to build railroads across their land. Many of the crew killed the buffaloes the Indians needed for their living. But the Indians could not stop railroad building any more than they could stop the settlers and the miners. The United States was determined to have railroads stretching across the continent. The government thought that they were necessary to the nation's growth. Railroads would provide transportation for the settlers. And they would give cattle raisers a way to ship to urban centers the herds they had driven up the trails from Texas.

Construction of the first transcontinental railroad was actually a race between two companies. They were racing to see which one could lay more miles of track before they met. The Central Pacific, starting out from Sacramento, hired thousands of Chinese laborers to lay track through the Sierra Nevada Mountains. The Union Pacific, starting in Omaha, hired thousands of ex-soldiers and Irish immigrants to throw down track across the plains.

In 1869, the last spike was driven into the track. Two engines, one coming from the west and one from the east, clanked noses in Utah. The Atlantic Ocean was now one week's journey from the Pacific. Soon other railroads to the West were built. Among them were the Northern Pacific, the Southern Pacific, and the Atchison, Topeka, and Santa Fe.

---

1. Look at page 32, and then answer the following on a sheet of paper: What easternmost city was served by what railroad? How many railroads served the northernmost city? What were the names of the two longest railroads? What cities did they join?
2. Imagine that you're an Indian in the West between 1860 and 1890. Write two paragraphs explaining how American settlers affected your way of life.

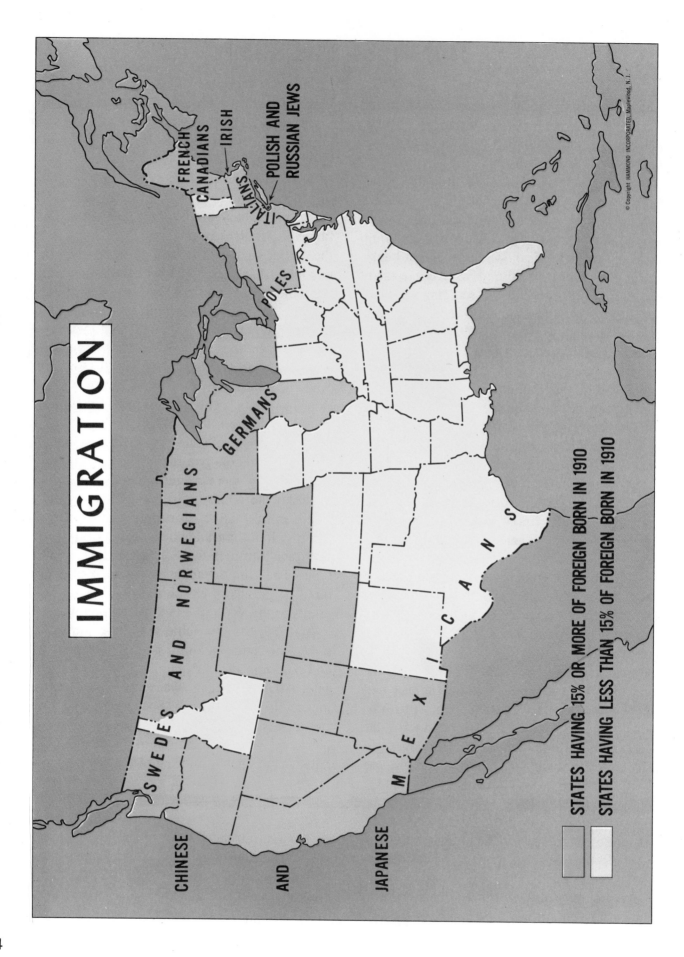

IMMIGRATION

FRENCH CANADIANS

IRISH

POLISH AND RUSSIAN JEWS

ITALIANS

POLES

GERMANS

SWEDES AND NORWEGIANS

CHINESE

AND

JAPANESE

MEXICANS

■ STATES HAVING 15% OR MORE OF FOREIGN BORN IN 1910

□ STATES HAVING LESS THAN 15% OF FOREIGN BORN IN 1910

© Copyright HAMMOND INCORPORATED, Maplewood, N. J.

IMMIGRATION

The growing American nation had both the room and the need for more citizens. There was land to be farmed. Factories needed workers to run the machines. There were railroads and canals to be built. There were minerals to be taken out of the earth.

American industries were growing at a time when troubles in other countries were making people eager to leave and build a new life elsewhere. Between 1820 and 1910, nearly 30 million of them left their place of birth and came to the United States.

The first groups to come were mainly from northern and western Europe. Among these were the Germans, Swedes, and Norwegians. Most of them had been farmers in their homelands. But many had lost their farms because of hard times. The United States called to them as a place where they could establish new farms. And so they came in great numbers in the middle and late 1800s. They settled across the northern row of states. Beginning in about 1860, more of the immigrants were skilled workers and experts. They were looking for jobs in the new industries that were springing up in the United States.

Farther to the east, French Canadians were settling in New Hampshire and Maine. They were in search of good farmland. Also, the lumbering industry offered work.

At about the same time, Ireland was having a terrible famine. Disease had attacked the mainstay of the Irish diet, the potato. Within six years, more than two million Irish people had either died of starvation or fled their country. Many of them came to the United States and settled along the northeastern seaboard. Unlike the Germans, Swedes, and Norwegians, they settled mainly in cities.

Throughout this period, the Chinese had been emigrating to the American west coast. The Japanese came later in the century. All sought to escape the poverty and lack of work in their homelands. The Chinese often took jobs as construction workers. The Japanese worked on farms and in small businesses.

The gaining of Texas and the rest of the Southwest from Mexico (during 1836-1848) brought many Mexicans into the United States. The Mexican Americans were often farmers. They also worked on large cattle ranches and in the gold mines.

Toward the end of the 1880s, large groups of immigrants began coming to the United States from southern and eastern Europe. The Italians and the Poles, for example, came because they could no longer get food to grow on their worn-out land. Religious persecution caused many Polish and Russian Jews to seek a country where they hoped to have religious freedom.

Many of the Italians and Jews settled along the northeastern seaboard. The Poles mainly went inland and settled in the Great Lakes region. In general, these people did not turn to farming. Instead, they looked for jobs as skilled or unskilled laborers.

As all of these various groups settled into life in the United States, they kept some of the flavor of their homelands. The combination of all these different flavors has given the United States a rich culture of its own.

1. America has often been called a "melting pot." Do you think this is an appropriate label for our nation? Explain your answer in two or more paragraphs.
2. Have you observed anything in your neighborhood which reflects a certain ethnic background? Discuss it in two paragraphs.
3. What are your "roots?" Write a short essay explaining why your ancestors may have come to this country.

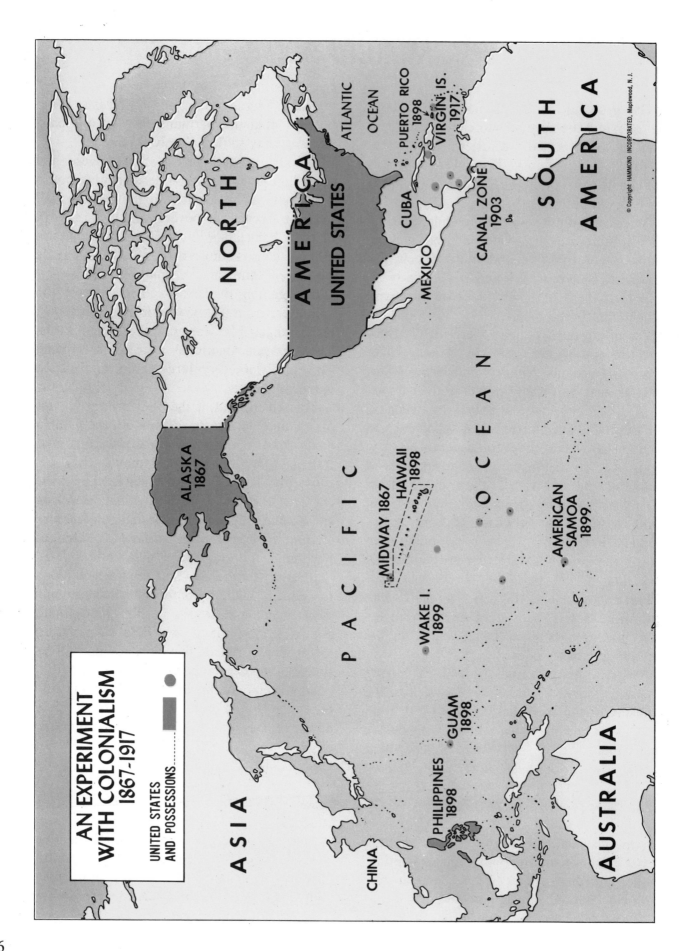

AN EXPERIMENT WITH COLONIALISM 1867-1917

UNITED STATES
AND POSSESSIONS ----------

NORTH AMERICA

UNITED STATES

ASIA

CHINA

PHILIPPINES
1898

GUAM
1898

WAKE I.
1899

MIDWAY 1867

HAWAII
1898

PACIFIC OCEAN

AMERICAN
SAMOA
1899

AUSTRALIA

ALASKA
1867

MEXICO

CUBA

ATLANTIC

OCEAN

PUERTO RICO
1898

VIRGIN IS.
1917

CANAL ZONE
1903

SOUTH AMERICA

© Copyright HAMMOND INCORPORATED, Maplewood, N.J.

AN EXPERIMENT WITH COLONIALISM

By the 1890s, the American frontier had almost disappeared. The United States was still interested in gaining more land, though.

Two steps in this direction had already been taken. In 1867, Secretary of State William Seward had convinced Congress to buy Alaska from Russia for $7,200,000. The purchase had been laughed at and called the "Million-Dollar Icebox" and "Seward's Folly." The United States not only bought Alaska, but in the same year, it took possession of the Midway Islands in the Pacific.

By 1899, Americans had changed their minds about Alaska. Gold was discovered in Nome. Thousands of people poured into "Seward's Folly" to strike it rich!

Early in 1898, an event occurred that caused the United States to gain territory in the Caribbean Sea. While Cuba was in revolt against Spain, the United States Ship *Maine* anchored in the harbor of Havana. In the night, an explosion ripped through the ship and killed 260 American seamen.

The cause of the explosion was never discovered. Yet some of the American press blamed the Spaniards. Within a short time, the United States declared war on Spain. The war was not fought in Spain or the United States, though. It was fought in Spanish overseas territories.

The Spanish-American War lasted only four months, and it was won by the Americans. As a result, the United States gained Puerto Rico in the Caribbean and the Philippine Islands and Guam in the Pacific. In return, Spain received $20 million. The Philippine Islands became independent after World War II.

The United States took more territory in the Pacific. American settlers in the Hawaiian Islands had long wanted the government to take over the islands. In 1898 they got their wish. The next year, the United States annexed two other places — Wake Island and part of the islands of Samoa.

The Spanish-American War showed the United States that its warships needed a quick route from the Atlantic Ocean to the Pacific. The government decided to build a canal through Central America. It would finish the one that the French had started in Panama. Since Panama was part of the Republic of Colombia, the United States offered to pay Colombia for use of the land the canal would run through. But the Colombians would not cooperate. The people of Panama wanted the canal. With the help and encouragement of France and the United States, the Panamanians revolted. They won, and the United States got the canal. (Later, the United States paid Colombia $25 million.)

The United States took one more territory in the Caribbean. Back in 1867, Seward had also tried to buy the Virgin Islands from Denmark, but Congress would not agree. Fifty years later, a more expansionist minded Congress wanted to buy. For $25 million, the United States bought three of the Virgin Islands.

---

1. Develop two or three paragraphs in which you discuss the question of American expansion as it might have been debated in the late 1800s and early 1900s.
2. Consult an encyclopedia or other reference source to learn the status of American Samoa and the Philippines shown as possessions on page 36. If their status has changed, explain the changes in writing on a separate sheet of paper.
3. Find Cuba on the map on page 36. What American territory lies south of Cuba?

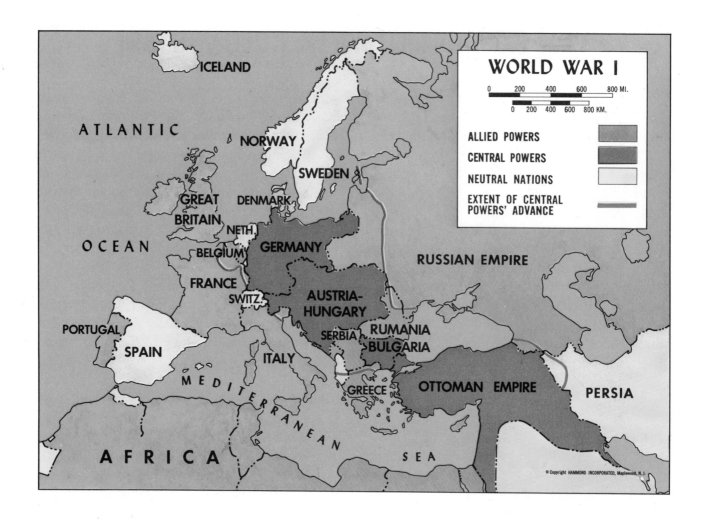

WORLD WAR I

For some time, there had been friction between Austria-Hungary and Serbia, neighboring nations. Many Serbs lived in Austria-Hungary and wanted to be united with Serbia. On July 28, 1914, the Archduke Francis Ferdinand, heir to Austria-Hungary's throne, was assassinated. Austria-Hungary blamed Serbia and declared war on that nation. Because of alliances, nation after nation was drawn into the war.

Germany overran Belgium and drove toward Paris. However, the Germans were stopped, and they retreated to a line behind the Aisne River. From there, the Germans drove toward the ports on the English Channel, but were stopped in a battle at Ypres. From that point, the Western Front bogged down to trench warfare. Poison gasses, modern machine guns, and the first use of tanks killed millions.

In 1917, the United States entered the war on the side of the Allied Powers. The fresh American troops and supplies tipped the scale in favor of the Allied Powers. One by one, the Central Powers lost the will to fight.

1. Some historians claim that the terms of the armistice that Germany was forced to sign were an important cause of World War II. Study the terms of the armistice and write a short, persuasive paper giving your opinion.

2. Poison gasses caused so much suffering and death on both sides that they were banned by all nations in World War II. Do you think that modern chemical warfare, germ warfare, napalm, and nuclear weapons should also be banned in all warfare? Write a short, persuasive paper supporting your opinion.

WORLD WAR II IN EUROPE (map legend)
- ALLIED NATIONS
- AXIS NATIONS
- AXIS OCCUPIED AREAS
- VICHY FRANCE
- NEUTRAL NATIONS
- MAJOR ALLIED ADVANCES

WORLD WAR II IN EUROPE

World War II in Europe began after militaristic dictatorships gained control of Germany and Italy. These dictatorships grew out of poor economic conditions in those countries.

In his rise to power, Adolph Hitler, the German dictator, used Jewish citizens as scapegoats for the nation's problems and to unite non-Jews in Germany against a common enemy. The result, after the war began, was the Holocaust. Millions of Jews died in this most shameful event in modern history.

Look at the map and note those nations that were Allied Powers, those that were Axis Powers, and those that were neutral. (Vichy France was a French government that cooperated with Germany after the fall of France.)

World War II began with lightning quickness, when Germany invaded Poland on September 1, 1939. Both England and France, which had defense agreements with Poland, declared war on Germany. On May 10, 1940, the Germans invaded the Netherlands and Belgium, and by May 13 had turned south behind the Maginot Line, a French fortification. German tanks rushed across France toward the English Channel, cutting off many Allied troops. A heroic effort by British military and civilian seamen evacuated many Allied soldiers from Dunkirk to England.

In December 1941, the United States entered the war. Fresh American troops and weapons were a welcome addition to the Allied war effort.

The Allies invaded North Africa, Sicily, Italy, and France, in that order. Italy surrendered first. Germany surrendered unconditionally on May 7, 1945.

1. Research the Holocaust. Write a report explaining why this event should be labeled "the most shameful event in modern history."
2. Draw an outline map of France, the Netherlands, and Belgium. Study the movements of the German army between May 10 and May 26. Trace and date these movements on your map.

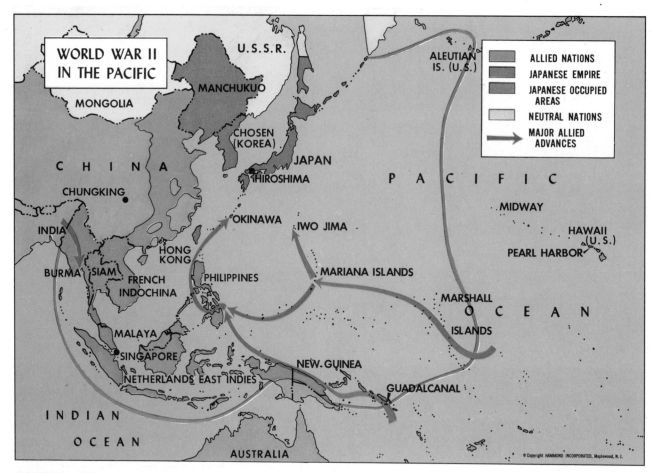

WORLD WAR II IN THE PACIFIC

On December 7, 1941, Japanese aircraft attacked the American Naval Station at Pearl Harbor, Hawaii, causing massive damage to the Pacific Fleet. Fortunately, the American aircraft carriers were not in the harbor when the attack came.

The Japanese then turned their attention to attacking and invading other American possessions in the Pacific. U. S. Intelligence "cracked" the Japanese military codes, giving us our only advantage over Japanese superiority in soldiers and weapons.

On June 4, 1942, using the broken code information, the U.S. Navy followed the progress of a huge Japanese fleet toward Midway Island. The Japanese did not think that American naval vessels were in the area. However, an American task force was nearby. The air battle which followed cost the Americans one carrier, but all four Japanese aircraft carriers involved in the battle were sunk. After Midway, the tide of the war turned.

American ground forces began an "island-hopping" attack with the capture of Guadalcanal in August. "Island-hopping" involved attacking major islands while bypassing the less important ones. Two of the most important islands to fall were Iwo Jima and Okinawa in 1945. With the capture of Okinawa, the Americans were only 350 miles from Japan.

On August 6, 1945, the U.S. dropped an atomic bomb on Hiroshima and 3 days later, another on Nagasaki, causing an enormous loss of life. On September 2, 1945, the Japanese surrendered aboard the U.S.S. *Missouri*, anchored in Tokyo Bay.

1. Although many brave American pilots died in the Battle of Midway, a small group of pilots turned the tide of battle. Read about the battle. Find out why this statement is true.

2. President Truman's decision to drop the atomic bomb was very difficult. What would you have done? Discuss your opinions in class.

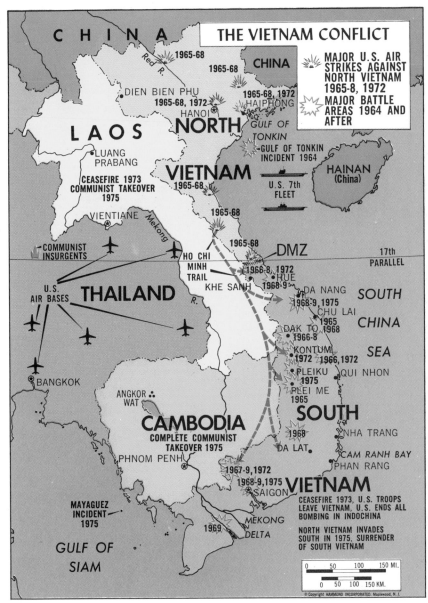

THE VIETNAM CONFLICT

MAJOR U.S. AIR STRIKES AGAINST NORTH VIETNAM 1965-8, 1972

MAJOR BATTLE AREAS 1964 AND AFTER

THE KOREAN WAR 1950-1953

THE KOREAN WAR

In 1950, without warning, Communist North Korea attacked South Korea. On one side was South Korea, the United States, and 15 other members of the United Nations. On the other side, North Korea was eventually joined by Communist China. The war ended in 1953, with a demilitarized zone being established near the 38th parallel, the original dividing line between the two Koreas.

THE VIETNAM CONFLICT

The United States became committed slowly to the fighting in Vietnam. In time, we were heavily involved in a war that cost the lives of 47,572 Americans. Our wounded, requiring hospitalization, totaled 153,329. Highlights of the war are shown on the map. Note which countries took part in the war. Thailand remained neutral, but permitted the U.S. to build bases there.

In 1973, the U.S. pulled out of the conflict. South Vietnam fell to Communist North Vietnam in 1975.

1. The American people supported our involvement in Korea. Yet the nation was divided over Vietnam. Research these statements. In no more than five paragraphs, explain them.

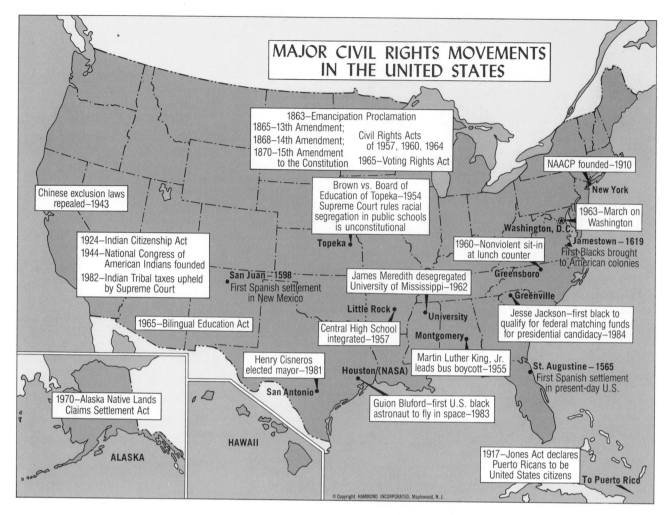

MAJOR CIVIL RIGHTS MOVEMENTS IN THE UNITED STATES

Even in this century, black Americans in many states were often segregated in schools, restaurants, and public waiting rooms. Further, although most states did not legally separate the races, many black Americans were in fact segregated in ghettos. Blacks earned less money than whites, had fewer educational opportunities, and found rewarding employment more difficult to obtain. This segregation that occurred, even though laws did not exist to separate the races, is called "de facto segregation."

Look at the map and note the important dates and events in the black civil rights movement. Notice that since 1955, important events have moved rapidly. Today, many black Americans are moving ahead, individually breaking down social and economic barriers.

Cubans who escaped Castro's Communist government have settled mostly in Florida and large eastern cities. Puerto Ricans, who are American citizens, move in large numbers be-tween Puerto Rico and cities in the Northeast and Midwest. Americans of Mexican ancestry still live in the Southwest from Texas to California, land that once belonged to Mexico. More recently, many Hispanic people have moved to the United States from Spanish-speaking South American nations. All Hispanic groups have at times faced prejudice in a nation whose primary language is English.

1. Notice that the Chinese exclusion laws were repealed in 1943. Trace the history of these laws and discuss them in class.
2. If the Indians were the first Americans, why did Congress pass the Indian Citizenship Act in 1924? Was this law necessary? Write three paragraphs giving your opinion.
3. Write a short biography of one of the following famous minority persons: Jesse Jackson, Shirley Chisholm, S. I. Hayakawa, Cesar Estrada Chavez, Luiz Munoz Marin, or Chief Joseph.

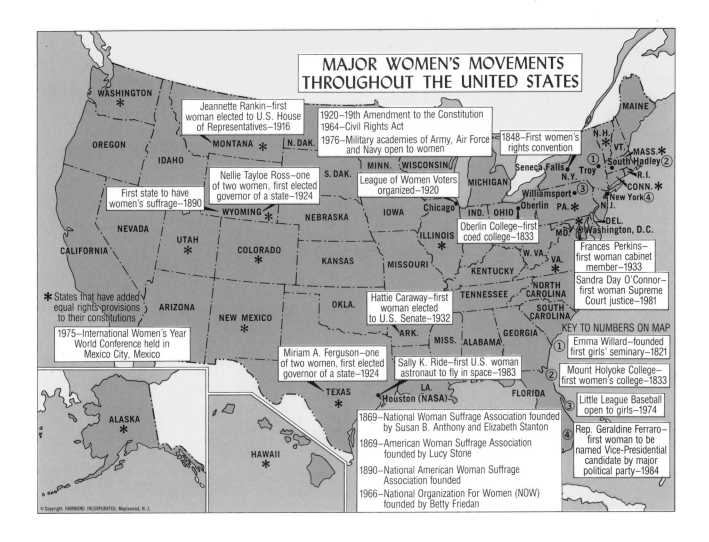

MAJOR WOMEN'S MOVEMENTS THROUGHOUT THE UNITED STATES

The map highlights important events in the fight for women's rights. Included are truly momentous events such as passage of the 19th Amendment to the Constitution, which gave women their long-overdue right to vote. Other events include important "firsts". Among these "firsts" are the first woman governor, U. S. senator, House member, and cabinet member. A recent entry includes the confirmation in 1981 of Sandra Day O'Connor as the first woman justice of the U.S. Supreme Court.

In 1972, an Equal Rights Amendment for women (ERA), was introduced and received the necessary two-thirds vote of both houses of Congress required for a proposal to amend the Constitution. Ratification by 38 states was then needed. By the deadline (March 22, 1979), only 35 of the required 38 states had ratified the ERA. The deadline was extended by Congress until June 30, 1982. At the end of the extension, the number of ratifying states remained at 35, thus killing the ERA.

The ERA effort cannot be considered a total defeat for those who advocated its passage. As the asterisks on map indicate, many states recognized the importance of clearly stating equality of the sexes and have added amendments to their state constitutions forbidding discrimination on the basis of gender.

1. Write three persuasive paragraphs in favor of, or opposed to, an ERA in the U.S. Constitution.
2. Write a short biography on the life of one of the women named on the map or one of the leaders of NOW.
3. Hold a class or group discussion entitled: What effects would the passage of an ERA have on the lives of American women legally, socially, and personally?

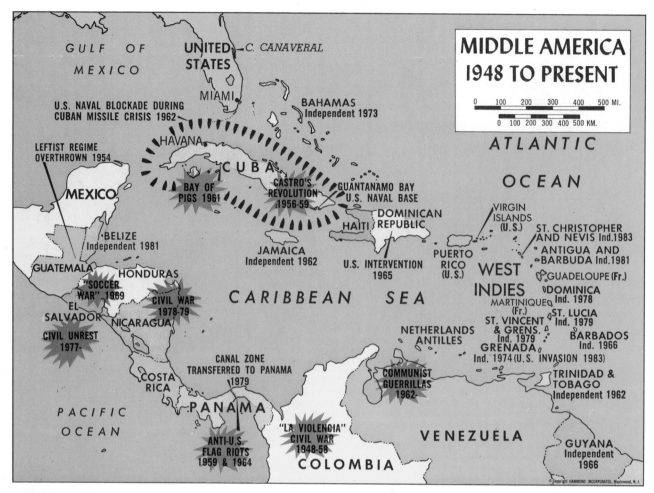

MIDDLE AMERICA 1948 TO PRESENT

Since Cuba's drift into Communism, that country has attempted to spread its revolution.

In 1979, Anastasio Somoza Debayle, the dictator of Nicaragua, was overthrown by members of the Sandinist National Liberation Front (FSLN). The nation was then ruled by a junta (a group of leaders). The United States sent much-needed food to the Nicaraguans. Within a year, however, the new government began to lean toward the Cuban Communists. Then, evidence began to indicate that Nicaragua might be aiding left-wing guerrillas trying to overthrow the government of neighboring El Salvador. In 1981, the U.S. suspended all aid to Nicargua. Nicaragua, in turn, began to seek more aid from Cuba, Mexico, Libya, and Communist Eastern Europe.

The government of El Salvador has been fighting well-armed, left-wing rebels. Their supplies, according to U.S. Intelligence, are coming from Cuba and are moving into El Salvador through Nicaragua. Because of this, the U.S. has steadily increased military aid to El Salvador. Many Americans, however, are opposed to this aid unless El Salvador improves human rights in that country.

Cuban adventurism also spread to Grenada, a Caribbean island. In the fall of 1983, a revolutionary group overthrew the government of Grenada. President Reagan was concerned about the safety of American medical students studying there. On October 25, 1983, the U.S. and six Caribbean nations invaded the island and evacuated the students. Over 600 Cubans were captured and large stores of Soviet-made arms were found.

1. Research the attack on Grenada. Write no more than five paragraphs describing the sequence of events.
2. Research Cuban activities in Central America and the Caribbean. Also study poverty in these areas. Have a debate entitled "The Cause of Political Unrest: Cuba or Poverty."

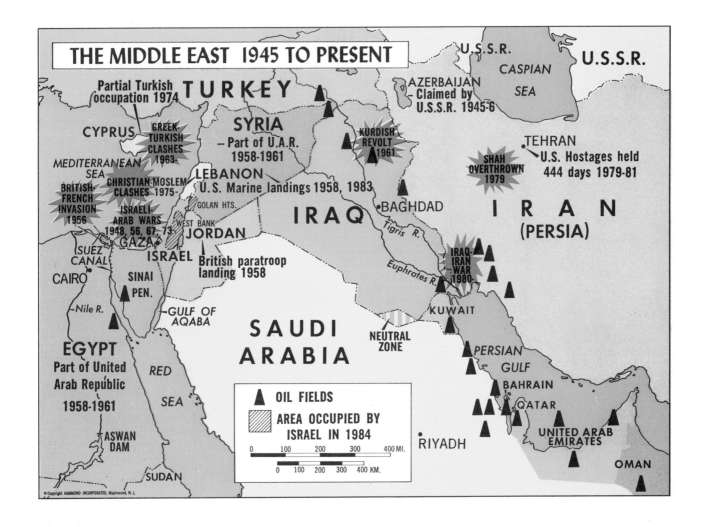

THE MIDDLE EAST 1945 TO PRESENT

Partial Turkish occupation 1974
TURKEY
SYRIA — Part of U.A.R. 1958-1961
CYPRUS
GREEK-TURKISH CLASHES 1963
KURDISH REVOLT 1961
U.S.S.R.
AZERBAIJAN — Claimed by U.S.S.R. 1945-6
CASPIAN SEA
U.S.S.R.
MEDITERRANEAN SEA
CHRISTIAN-MOSLEM CLASHES 1975-
LEBANON
U.S. Marine landings 1958, 1983
GOLAN HTS.
TEHRAN
SHAH OVERTHROWN 1979
U.S. Hostages held 444 days 1979-81
BRITISH-FRENCH INVASION 1956
ISRAELI-ARAB WARS 1948, 56, 67, 73
WEST BANK
BAGHDAD
IRAQ
Tigris R.
I R A N (PERSIA)
SUEZ CANAL
GAZA
JORDAN
ISRAEL
British paratroop landing 1958
Euphrates R.
IRAQ-IRAN WAR 1980
CAIRO
Nile R.
SINAI PEN.
GULF OF AQABA
SAUDI ARABIA
NEUTRAL ZONE
KUWAIT
EGYPT
Part of United Arab Republic 1958-1961
RED SEA
PERSIAN GULF
BAHRAIN
QATAR
UNITED ARAB EMIRATES
OMAN
ASWAN DAM
SUDAN
RIYADH

▲ OIL FIELDS
▨ AREA OCCUPIED BY ISRAEL IN 1984
0 100 200 300 400 MI.
0 100 200 300 400 KM.

© Copyright HAMMOND INCORPORATED, Maplewood, N. J.

THE MIDDLE EAST 1945 TO PRESENT

Look at the border between Iraq and Iran on the map. The armies of these two Middle Eastern nations have swept back and forth over this area, with enormous casualties on both sides since 1980. What began as a border dispute led to a full-scale invasion of Iran in September 1980. Iraq drove deep into Western Iran. In 1982, Iran counterattacked and drove the Iraqis from Iran. Both nations have bombed civilian population centers. Most recently, Iraqi and Iranian fighter planes have attacked neutral tankers in the Persian Gulf in order to disrupt the flow of each other's oil.

Find Lebanon on the map. Throughout the history of Lebanon, tensions have existed between Christian and Moslem citizens. This tension increased in the 1970s, when the Moslem Palestine Liberation Organization guerrillas under Yasir Arafat moved into Lebanon. Palestinian guerrillas began making raids against northern Israel. Finally, in 1982

Israel invaded Lebanon and drove all the way to Beirut, destroying Palestinian strongholds. Israel agreed to pull its forces back in return for American, British, Italian, and French peace-keeping forces. During this period, a terrorist bomb attack led to the death of over 200 U.S. Marines. In time, the peace-keeping forces were withdrawn, and Lebanon still remains torn between Christian, Moslem, Syrian, and Israeli interests.

1. Research the events that led to the establishment of the state of Israel in 1948. In no more than six paragraphs, describe the sequence of events that led to an independent Israel.
2. From 1958 to 1961, Egypt and Syria were joined as the United Arab Republic. Why did this union not last? Study this period and discuss it in class.

MAP INDEX